players and painted stage
the theatre of w.b. yeats

karen dorn

THE HARVESTER PRESS • SUSSEX
BARNES & NOBLE BOOKS • NEW JERSEY

First published in Great Britain in 1984 by
THE HARVESTER PRESS LIMITED
Publisher: John Spiers
16 Ship Street, Brighton, Sussex
and in the USA by
BARNES & NOBLE BOOKS
81, Adams Drive, Totowa, New Jersey 07512

© Karen Dorn, 1984

British Library Cataloguing in Publication Data

Dorn, Karen
Players and painted stage.
   1. Yeats, W. B. — Dramatic works
 I. Title
822'.8   PR 5908.D7

ISBN 0-7108-0595-0

Library of Congress Cataloging in Publication Data

Dorn, Karen.
  Players and painted stage.

   1. Yeats, W. B. (William Butler), 1865-1939 — Dramatic works.
2. Yeats, W. B. (William Butler), 1865-1939 — Stage history.
I. Title.
PR 5908.D7D67   1984   822'.8   83-7140
ISBN 0-389-20413-7

Photoset in 11 on 12 point Times by Alacrity Phototypesetters,
Banwell Castle, Weston-super-Mare.
Printed in Great Britain by
Biddles Limited, Guildford, Surrey

All rights reserved

And when the Fool and the Blind Man stole the bread
Cuchulain fought the ungovernable sea;
Heart-mysteries there, and yet when all is said
It was the dream itself enchanted me:
Character isolated by a deed
To engross the present and dominate memory.
Players and painted stage took all my love,
And not those things they were emblems of.

                from 'The Circus Animals' Desertion'

Contents

	List of Illustrations	ix
	Preface	xi
I	Stage Images and the 'National Argument': W. B. Yeats's Play *Deirdre* and the Early Abbey Theatre Controversy	1
II	Dialogue into Movement: Yeats's Theatre Collaboration with Gordon Craig	13
III	An Intimate Theatre: The Japanese Noh Drama and Yeats's Dance Plays	34
IV	Stage Production and the Greek Theatre Movement: W. B. Yeats's Play *The Resurrection*, and his Versions of *King Oedipus*, and *Oedipus at Colonus*	63
V	The New Dance Drama: Yeats's Last Dance Plays	83
	Notes	97
	Select Bibliography	127
	Sources of Illustrations	133
	Acknowledgements	135
	Index	137

List of Illustrations

1. A stage design for W. B. Yeats's *Deirdre*, 1906, by Robert Gregory.
2. The old Empire Music Hall, Newcastle.
3. a. Serlio's wood engraving *Scena Tragica*, 1566.
   b. Gordon Craig's first drawing for *Scene*, 1906.
4. A moment of arrested motion in Gordon Craig's conception of *Scene*.
5. Gordon Craig with his model stage, London 1910.
6. Robert Gregory's design for the original 1903 production W. B. Yeats's *The Hour-Glass*.
7. A page from W. B. Yeats's Notebook of Scene Arrangements, 1910, showing a floor plan for Gordon Craig's screens for *The Hour-Glass*.
8. Mask of the Blind Man for W. B. Yeats's *On Baile's Strand*, wood engraving by Gordon Craig, 1911.
9. Stage setting for *The Hour-Glass*, by Gordon Craig, 1911.
10. Mask of the Fool for *The Hour-Glass*, by Gordon Craig, 1911.
11. Costume of the Fool for *The Hour-Glass*, by Gordon Craig, 1911.
12. Backcloth for W. B. Yeats's *The King's Threshold*, Jack B. Yeats, 1913.
13. Design for Cuchulain's costume in W. B. Yeats's *On Baile's Strand*, 1915, by Charles Ricketts.
14. Michio Itoh in the costume of the Guardian of the Well in W. B. Yeats's *At the Hawk's Well*, 1916.
15. Cloth for *At the Hawk's Well*, 1916, by Edmund Dulac.
16. Masked actors in the 1926 Amsterdam production of W. B. Yeats's *The Only Jealousy of Emer*.
17. 'In Italy: Design for a Scene', wood engraving by Gordon Craig, 1907.

Players and Painted Stage

18 'Hamlet: An Actor', wood engraving by Gordon Craig, 1912.
19 'Hamlet and Daemon', wood engraving by Gordon Craig, 1909.
20 Gordon Craig's model stage setting for Stanislavski's production of *Hamlet*, Moscow Art Theatre, 1911.
21 'Troy Burning', wood engraving by Gordon Craig, 1908.
22 E. W. Godwin's stage design for *Helen of Troy*, Hengler's Circus, London, 1886.
23 Max Reinhardt's production of *Oedipus Rex*, Schumann Circus, Berlin, 1910.
24 Max Reinhardt's production of *Oedipus Rex*, Covent Garden, London, 1912.
25 The old Abbey Theatre's proscenium stage and orchestra pit.
26 The stage setting for W. B. Yeats's *King Oedipus*, Abbey Theatre, Dublin, 1926.
27 Stage setting at the Festival Theatre, Cambridge, 1930.
28 Backcloth for W. B. Yeats's *Fighting the Waves*, by D. Travers Smith, 1929.
29 Cuchulain's dance in *Fighting the Waves*, Abbey Theatre, Dublin, 1929.
30 Hildo Krop's Mask of Fand, used in *Fighting the Waves*, 1929.
31 The masks and costumes for two Dublin productions of W. B. Yeats's *The King of the Great Clock Tower*.
32 The stage and stalls of the Mercury Theatre, London.

Preface

This book is a study of W. B. Yeats's work as an experimenter and contributor to the modern theatre. Yeats's long involvement with drama in performance illustrated his belief that the poet is a maker of images — images which in the theatre can be expanded into a whole built from language, actors' movements, and stage settings.

During fifty years of writing and producing plays, Yeats was involved in some of the most innovative theatre of the early twentieth century. When he began, the radical theatre style was the naturalism of the 'social dramas' of Ibsen, Strindberg, and Shaw. Yeats's objections to that style led to his work in establishing the Abbey Theatre in 1904 and in attempting to create a nonnaturalistic drama based on Irish legend. Though the Abbey did not develop according to Yeats's plan, his subsequent work with the theatre designer Gordon Craig gave him valuable experience, which led in turn to the creation of his plays for dancers. This new form of drama, adated from the Japanese dance drama, was designed for small audiences attending drawing room performances. In his later work, however, he returned to full state productions. His popular versions of Sophocles' Oedipus plays were the culmination of his long involvement with the revival of Greek drama began by Gilbert Murray and Granville Barker. In his final work, Yeats created a new form combining dance, dialogue, and music in his collaboration with Diaghilev's dancer, Ninette de Valois, and the London experimental theatres of poetic drama. Yeats was greatly encouraged by the new productions and audiences, seeing in them the emergence of the theatre he had envisaged since his early days at the Abbey.

I have drawn on contemporary records of stage settings and costumes, some of which were first used at the Abbey Theatre and its experimental stage, the Peacock Theatre, in order to define the relation between stage design, performance, and the initiating dramatic form. My emphasis is rather more on dramatic form than poetic language, though strictly speaking the two aspects are inseparable in Yeats's plays. My own practical experience in matters of the theatre has thus been subordinated to this end, though I hope it will have made me alert to the theatrical implications of Yeats's writing, and that students of drama will find the documentation of use. Yeats's nondramatic works are an essential support to any reading of the plays, and I have drawn attention to the important studies of the plays as literature. The chapters are arranged roughly chronologically in order to follow the development of Yeats's work in connection with cross-currents in the European theatre. While this approach results in certain lines of inquiry being sketched in rather than drawn in depth, as in a more specialized study, my intention is to include the wide range of interests that have animated twentieth-century theatre — the controversy surrounding naturalistic drama, the inspiration of classical Greek and Japanese dramatic forms, the shaping influence of new approaches to stage settings, and the fascination with the expressive figure of the dancer. The detailed readings of passages from Yeats's plays are used to show how the complete stage image is built up to embody theme and action. Yeats's drama was a blend of many kinds, drawing its full life from performance at a time when such a combination of poetic power and theatrical experience was rare, if not unique.

I first looked at Yeats's plays after reading Susanne K. Langer's discussions of expressive form in *Philosophy in a New Key*. My particular concern was with the interaction between dramatic form and stage performance, though at that time Yeats's plays were studied primarily as literary texts. Since then a number of studies have appeared that indicate a radical change in the critical and scholarly approaches to Yeats's drama, and I should like to mention some of these. Peter Ure's *Yeats the Playwright* (1963) and David R. Clark's *W.B. Yeats and the Theatre of Desolate Reality* (1965) marked a transition from the previous literary approach. In *Masks of Love and*

Preface

Death: Yeats as Dramatist (1971), John Rees Moore considered the plays in the light of Yeats's plan to create an heroic national drama embodied in ritual; more recent work by George Mills Harper and Kathleen Raine has shown Yeats's involvement in the creation of ceremony and ritual for the Golden Dawn. The inspiration of the Japanese Noh theatre upon Yeats's dance plays, a major area of interest, has been the subject of two recent books: Akhtar Qamber's *Yeats and the Noh* (1974) emphasizes the importance of a cultural and social bond between audience and performance; Richard Taylor's detailed study of Yeats's assimilation of Noh technique through the agency of Ernest Fenollosa and Ezra Pound, *The Drama of W. B. Yeats: Irish Myth and the Japanese Nō* (1976), distinguishes between the philosophy and dramatic form of the Noh and Yeats's selective adaptations. In addition, new approaches to Yeats's revisions have been made possible through the publication of manuscript material. David R. Clark's series, *Manuscripts of W. B. Yeats*, will be invaluable; the volumes already published include *Druid Craft: The Writing of The Shadowy Waters* (1971), edited by M. J. Sidnell, G. P. Mayhew and David R. Clark, and *W. B. Yeats: The Writing of The Player Queen* (1977), edited by Curtis Bradford. The first volume of the Yeats Studies Series, *Yeats and the Theatre* (1975), edited by Robert O'Driscoll and Lorna Reynolds, contains previously unpublished lectures and typescripts of Yeats's versions of Sophocles (the essays include chapter 2 of the present study). Finally, several books have been written by people whose experience in the production of Yeats's plays has perhaps at last put to rest the prejudice that Yeats was not a man of the theatre. Reg Skene's *The Cuchulain Plays of W. B. Yeats* (1974) is a presentation of the Cuchulain cycle in the light of his own productions and Yeats's view of ritual in dramatic performance. James W. Flannery's *W. B. Yeats and the Idea of a Theatre: The Early Abbey Theatre in Theory and Practice* (1976) documents the development of Yeats's views of dramatic form and the function of a national theatre. Liam Miller's beautiful book, *The Noble Drama of W. B. Yeats* (1977), illustrated by reproductions of original stage settings and costumes, will become a standard reference for those who are interested in Yeats's knowledge of theatre production. Katharine Worth's

Players and Painted Stage

The Irish Drama of Europe from Yeats to Beckett (1978) emphasizes the European context of Yeats's drama and records the recent productions of Yeats's plays, including her own, now available on video tape. Her account of London theatre and dance in the 1970s is a lively tribute to 'The Vitality of the Yeatsian Theatre'.

I
Stage Images and the 'National Argument': W.B. Yeats's Play Deirdre *and* the Early Abbey Theatre Controversy

When W.B. Yeats was working on *The Player Queen* in 1910, he used a small model stage (Plate 5) made for him by the theatre designer Gordon Craig. The materials Yeats used — masks, folding screens, the play of light and shadow across geometric forms — would be recognised as part of theatre convention by a young spectator today. Had his grandfather sought out the small arts theatres of the early twentieth century, or his grandmother sat through rehearsals of verse-speaking in a draughty hall, things would have appeared in quite a different light. At that time the arts theatre, or what Norman Marshall has called 'the Other Theatre,' was the work of a small group of actors, writers, and producers vehemently opposed to the increasingly dominant form of drama. Variously described as 'naturalism' or 'realism',[1] that form of drama was part of the growing interest during the latter half of the nineteenth century in the local, anecdotal, and biographical aspect of the arts, as opposed to the general and typical. The period was one of an increasing sense of national identity, and from the music of Sibelius to the 'social drama' of Ibsen, Strindberg, Hauptmann, or the paintings of the French Impressionists, great emphasis was given to the creation of a picture of reality from local or national characteristics. As Monet's paintings of Rouen Cathedral recorded the changing light of day, the work of the naturalists offered a wide range of views. The fierce arguments attending each new production of naturalistic drama turned on one question — the extent to which the 'slice of life' corresponded with life outside the theatre, whether the life of the middle classes depicted in Ibsen's plays and later in the English plays, or the working classes in early German realism, or the Irish peasantry in the work of the Abbey Theatre.

The early years of the Abbey have been a subject of keen interest, a crystallisation of the issues underlying early-twentieth-century theatre.[2] Established in Dublin in 1904 by Lady Gregory, John Millington Synge, Yeats, and the Fay brothers' Irish players, with financial support from Miss Annie Horniman, the Abbey reflected the debate surrounding the campaign for Home Rule and the emerging Irish nationalism. In particular, the argument concerned the extent to which the Abbey could influence, through its choice of plays, the growing national identity. Describing the controversy surrounding Lady Gregory's *The Rising of the Moon* in 1907, Yeats wrote:

> A little play, The Rising of the Moon, ... has ... roused the suspicions of a very resolute leader of the people, who has a keen eye for rats behind the arras. A Fenian ballad-singer partly converts a policeman, and is it not unwise under any circumstances to show a policeman in so favourable a light? It is well known that many of the younger policemen were Fenians: but it is necessary that the Dublin crowds should be kept of so high a heart that they will fight the police at any moment. Are not morals greater than literature?[3]

Yeats continued:

> Others have objected to Mr. Synge's *Shadow of the Glen* because Irish women, being more chaste than those of England and Scotland, are a valuable part of our National argument.[4]

Abbey opponents might insist on the dramatis personae of the chaste young woman, virtuous Irish wife, proud patriot, pious Catholic, and anti-Irish police, but Yeats replied that 'sometimes the patriot will have to falter and the wife to desert her home, and neither be followed by divine vengeance or man's judgement.'[5] Spectators rejected the brutal naturalism in Synge's portrayal of western Ireland in *The Playboy of the Western World* (1906) and the unorthodox Christianity in Yeats's *The Countess Cathleen* (1899), while his *Cathleen ni Houlihan* (1902) was immensely popular for its evocation of a passionate nationalism. 'In using what I considered traditional symbols,' Yeats later recalled, 'I forgot that in Ireland they are not symbols but realities.'[6]

Stage Images and the 'National Argument'

As playwright and manager, Yeats worked closely with the Abbey in extending its representation of contemporary Irish life. While he supported its naturalistic drama, especially the work of Synge, his plans for the Abbey encompassed a wider range of material — the little-known tradition of Irish legends and folk tales. His early work was a development of a style of presentation suitable to that tradition. For his purposes, naturalism was too limited in its emphasis on the external and superficial aspects of character and action. His autobiographical essay, 'The Tragic Generation,' records the debate over language and stage setting provoked by the first naturalistic productions in London. Ibsen's *A Doll's House* (1894), condemned by one critic as a 'series of conversations terminated by an accident,' was in Yeats's view an invitation 'to admire dialogue so close to modern educated speech that music and style were impossible.'[7] *The Land of Heart's Desire*, the first of Yeats's plays to be produced, shared the bill in 1894 with George Bernard Shaw's *Arms and the Man*, a play that seemed to Yeats an 'inorganic, logical straightness and not the crooked road of life.'[8] When the Abbey was established a few years later, Yeats's chief opponent was George Moore, a great defender of Ibsen and the European naturalistic drama. As Yeats wrote, 'I saw Moore daily, we were at work on *Diarmuid and Grania*. Lady Gregory thought such collaboration would injure my art, and was perhaps right. Because his mind was argumentative, abstract, diagrammatic, mine sensuous, concrete, rhythmical, we argued about words.'[9] In 'Discoveries' (1906), Yeats clarified his disagreement with Moore and the restrictions of naturalism:

Tha happiest writers are those that, knowing this form of play to be slight and passing, keep to the surface, never showing anything but the arguments and the persiflage of daily observation, or now and then, instead of the expression of passion, a stage picture, a man holding a woman's hand or sitting with his head in his hands in dim light by the red glow of a fire. It was certainly an understanding of the slightness of the form, or its capacity for the expression of the deeper sorts of passion, that made the French invent the play with a thesis, for where there is a thesis people can grow hot in argument, almost the only kind of passion that displays itself in our daily life.[10]

The opposition of newspapers and literary and political

societies to the Abbey Theatre — opposition both to its controversial naturalistic productions and its interpretation of Irish legends — can best be summed up in the argument directed specifically at its playwrights. If Ireland's literature, her songs and theatre, were to be a source of political unity, what was *Irish* literature? Should it be written by Irishmen or by Anglo-Irishmen, in Gaelic or English? Yeats answered the question by broadening its reference. Anglo-Irish himself and with no knowledge of Gaelic, he was willing 'to extend his interpretation of Anglo-Irish letters not only to embrace his good friends Lionel Johnson and Arthur Symons, but to sense an undefined Celtic sympathy even in such opposite forces as William Blake and Maurice Maeterlinck.'[11] Against complaints that the Abbey neglected Gaelic plays and the Irish national cause, Yeats replied that national literature should be 'the work of writers who are moulded out of so deep a life that they are accepted there in the end.'[12] He saw little power in the images of nationalism offered by the Abbey's opponents. Newspapers and sermons gave only the 'personifications of averages, of statistics, or even personified opinions, or men and women so faintly imagined that there is nothing about them to separate them from the crowd, as it appears to our hasty eyes.'[13] Only the poet, Yeats thought, could 'name and number the passions and motives of men'; only literature, 'the great teaching power or the world,' could teach Ireland a greater image of herself.[14]

Yeats's early Abbey plays — *The Hour-Glass, The Shadowy Waters, The King's Threshold, On Baile's Strand, Deirdre, The Golden Helmet, The Green Helmet* — all reflect this view of literature as a great teaching power. Based on traditional tales, the plays vividly portray the importance Yeats placed on the imaginative life. The emphasis can be illustrated by the opening scene of *Deirdre*, in its dramatic form, its stage setting, and its dialogue. First produced in 1906, *Deirdre* was adapted from Lady Gregory's version of Irish heroic saga, *Cuchulain of Muirthemne*.[15] Yeats selected incidents from the final episodes of the tale: Deirdre's and Naoise's return after long exile, the King's treachery and the death of the two lovers. Through the use of choral interludes and the interweaving of fable and stage action, Yeats emphasised the nature of Deirdre's final choice

Stage Images and the 'National Argument'

to die with Naoise rather than remain as Queen, a choice based on the model of behaviour found in Irish heroic traditon. In the opening scene, the Musicians direct the spectators' attention to the crucial moment of the play:

> First Musician. I have a story right, my wanderers,
> That has so mixed with fable in our songs
> That all seemed fabulous.
> ....
> Second Musician. The tale were well enough
> Had it a finish. (171, 172)

As a visual representation of Deirdre's final choice, Yeats used a stage setting that takes on an increasingly symbolic quality as the stage properties are drawn into the action of the play. Robert Gregory's watercolour design (Plate 1) for the original production suggests the degree of stylisation: a large travelling tent set in a pattern of trees, a pre-Raphaelite secret rendezvous.[16] On the small Abbey stage, a cottage set was adapted to suggest an Irish landscape, a mysterious outer world glimpsed through the familiar house.

A guest house in a wood. It is a rough house of timber; through the doors and some of the windows one can see the great spaces of the wood, the sky dimming, night closing in. But a window to the left shows the thick leaves of a coppice; the landscape suggests silence and loneliness.[17]

The guest house lies near the seashore, a contrast based on Yeats's central images of sea and tower, symbolizing the natural life and the intellect, 'towers of thought's crowned powers.'[18] The contrast is carried over into the room itself. A burning brazier is placed opposite a small table with chess board and chessmen — the imagination, as it were, set against the logic and calculation of the intellect.[19]

The contrast embodied in the stage setting is made more explicit in the opening dialogue between the King's man Fergus and the Musicians. Their disagreement over the King's intention becomes in effect a dispute about politics and poetry. Fergus has the King's 'oath' for the pardon of the lovers and dismisses the women's 'gossip'. They 'slander' the King, their 'wild thought' fed on 'extravagant poetry.' Though he denies the truth of their 'fabulous tales,' Fergus reveals his suspicion as he asks for a song:

> Begin, begin, of some old king and queen,
> Of Lugaidh Redstripe or another; no, not him,
> He and his lady perished wretchedly. (176)

The Musicians sing of passion, vividly imagined as a turbulent bird buffeted by the wind, and their lyric draws together the tales of Edain and Aillinn, who followed passion beyond death, transformed into the shape of birds.[20]

> 'Why is it', Queen Edain said,
>   'If I do but climb the stair
> To the tower overhead,
>   When the winds are calling there,
> Or the gannets calling out
>   In waste places of the sky,
> There's so much to think about
>   That I cry, that I cry?'
>
> But her good man answered her:
>   'Love would be a thing of naught
> Had not all his limgs a stir
>   Born out of immoderate thought;
> Were he anything by half,
>   Were his measure running dry.
> Lovers, if they may not laugh,
>   Have to cry, have to cry.'

As Deirdre and Naiose enter, the final lines of the song join them with the other lovers:

> But is Edain worth a song
>   Now the hunt begins anew?
> Praise the beautiful and strong;
>   Praise the redness of the yew;
> Praise the blossoming apple-stem.
>   But our silence had been wise.
> What is all our praise to them
>   That have one another's eyes? (177-178)

The opening episode, then, presents the matter of the play, what Barton Friedman calls the 'myth-making process.'[21] Naoise and Deirdre will reenact the old tale, love will become desire for death. Yeats's play, though radically different in theme and form from contemporary naturalistic drama, was nevertheless intended as a representation of contemporary life.

In its opposition between poetry and politics, expressed both in dialogue and structure, Yeats's *Deirdre* was directed in

Stage Images and the 'National Argument'

part towards the Abbey's detractors. In his view, 'Neither the grammars of the Gaelic League nor the industrialism of the *Leader*, nor the *Sinn Fein* attacks upon the Irish Party, give sensible images to the affections.' No 'national feeling,' no 'idea of a nation,' could develop without 'a model of it in the mind of the people.[22] *Deirdre* was part of the plan underlying Yeats's Abbey work, as set out in his 1909 diary: 'When I was twenty-five or twenty-six I planned a *Legende des Siecles* of Ireland that was to set out with my *Wanderings of Oisin*, and show something of every century. Lionel Johnson's work and, later, Lady Gregory's, carried on the dream in a different form; and I did not see, until Synge began to write, that we must denounce the deliberate creation of a kind of Holy City in the imagination, and express the individual.' 'Meanwhile,' Yeats continued, 'the need of a model of a nation, of some moral diagram is ... great.'[23] In *Deirdre*, the development of the action is governed not by political expediency but by the model of behaviour preserved in traditional literature. Deirdre and Naoise's moment of choice represents what Yeats later described as Ireland taking on an image of itself, as wax waiting for the seal. Recalling the period of the early Abbey, Yeats wrote that nations or individuals were united by the image that could evoke the most difficult state of mind 'because only the greatest obstacle that can be contemplated without despair rouses the will to full intensity.' If the Irish were 'declamatory, loose, and bragging, we were but the better fitted — that declared and measured — to create unyielding personality, manner at once cold and passionate, daring long-premeditated act.'[24] In *Deirdre* the movement towards the premeditated act is first built up through continual allusions, in the stage action and dialogue, to performing and role-playing. As the curtain opens, the Musicians are 'arraying themselves — the one holding a mirror for the other perhaps.' When Deirdre arrives, she reddens her cheeks and puts on the ruby necklace, but

>   Now wearing them
> Myself wars on myself, for I myself—
> That do my husband's will, yet fear to do it—
> Grow dragonish to myself.   (178)

As her suspicion of the King's treachery increases, she accuses

Naoise of speaking falsely, like a masked actor 'from the lips out,' attempting to force his escape by deceit:

> Look at my face where the leaf raddled it
> And at these rubies on my hair and breast.
> It was for him, to stir him to desire,
> I put on beauty; yes, for Conchubar. (185)

When Naoise hesitates, she tries another disguise:

> There is but one way to make all safe:
> I'll spoil this beauty that brought misery
> And houseless wandering on the man I loved.
> These wanderers will show me how to do it;
> To clip this hair to baldness, blacken my skin
> With walnut juice, and tear my face with briars.
> O that the creatures of the woods had torn
> My body with their claws! (186-187)

With the entrance of the King's Messenger, these allusions to role-playing are brought into direct action. Now Naoise sees that the King's arrival will bring death, not reconciliation. Earlier Deirdre seemed to have, in Naoise's words,

> the heart of the wild birds that fear
> The net of the fowler or the wicker cage. (184)

Now 'the crib has fallen'; he does not want to be 'beating in a vain fury at the cage's door.' One decision remains; how it is enacted constitutes the central 'moral diagram' of the play. The connection Yeats drew between stage characters and his Irish audience was set out in the 1909 diary as his 'theory of the Mask':

There is a relation between discipline and the theatrical sense. If we cannot imagine ourselves as different from what we are and assume that second self, we cannot impose a discipline upon ourselves, though we may accept one from others. Active virtue as distinguished from the passive acceptance of a current code is therefore theatrical, consciously dramatic, the wearing of a mask. It is the condition of arduous full life ....

I think that all happiness depends on the energy to assume the mask of some other self; that all joyous or creative life is a rebirth of something not oneself, something which has no memory and is created in a moment and perpetually renewed.[25]

Deirdre is a dramatization of Yeats's theory of the Mask, presented first as a tableau or play-within-a-play, and in the

Stage Images and the 'National Argument'

final moments as part of the main action. The tableau, a scene from the story of Lugaidh Redstripe and his seamew wife who awaited death playing chess, is enacted by the lovers when they see their own end. The Musicians' torches, lit from the brazier, brighten the room, emphasising the special imaginative quality of the scene. Naoise and Deirdre's chess game is accompanied by a song evoking the mood Yeats called 'at once cold and passionate.' The Musicians sing of the desire of lovers as a shadow of the great desire for ecstasy beyond death:[26]

> Love is an immoderate thing
> And can never be content
> Till it dip an ageing wing
> Where some laughing element
> Leaps and Time's old lanthorn dims.
> What's the merit in love-play,
> In the tumult of the limbs
> That dies out before 'tis day,
> Heart on heart, or mouth on mouth
> All that mingling of our breath,
> Where love-longing is but drouth
> For the things come after death? (191)

The role is difficult and Deirdre ends the tableau:

> I cannot go on playing like that woman
> That had but the cold blood of the sea in her veins. (191-192)

When Naoise urges her to 'take up your man again' she abandons the game of chess:

> Bend and kiss me now,
> For it may be the last before our death.
> And when that's over we'll be different;
> Imperishable things, a cloud or a fire.
> And I know nothing but this body, nothing
> But that old vehement, bewildering kiss. (192)

And at the sight of the King, Naoise too abandons the game:

> First Musician. He came to spy upon you, not to fight.
> Naoise. A prudent hunter, therefore, but no king.
> He'd find if what has fallen in the pit
> Were worth the hunting, but has come too near,
> And I turn hunter.... (192)

When the two men return, Naoise's image of the hunter is embodied in the full stage image: he is himself ensnared in the net.

In the final moments of the play, Deirdre takes up the role again. There is a further movement from speech to stage image, from rehearsal to action. Yeats's comment on Deirdre's performance — 'Red-heat up to Naisi's death, white-heat after he is dead'[27] — describes the shift from indecision to premeditated act. Early in the play, Deirdre and Naoise spoke of the colour gone from the other's cheek through foreknowledge of death; Lugaidh's seamew wife had 'the cold sea's blood in her.' This imagery of colour underlies Deirdre's final deception of the King when the Executioner returns with a sword covered in Naoise's blood:

> Although we are so delicately made,
> There's something brutal in us, and we are won
> By those who can shed blood. (199)

When the King hesitates,

> You are deceiving me.
> You long to look upon his face again.
> Why should I give you now to a dead man
> That took you from a living? (200)

Deirdre convinces him through subtle reversion to the imagery:

> For I will see him
> All blood be-dabbled and his beauty gone.
> It's better, when you're beside me in your strength,
> That the mind's eye should call up the soiled body,
> And not the shape I loved. (200)

The play ends in a second tableau, representing the triumph of heroic legend over the political subterfuge of the King. Deirdre steps behind the curtain hiding Naoise's body as the women sing the end:

> First Musician. Into the secret wilderness of their love.
>
> Second Musician. A high, grey cairn. What more is to be said?
>
> First Musician. Eagles have gone into their cloudy bed. (202)

Torches of approaching men, Naoise's supporters, light up the tableau as the lovers are discovered. Fergus links the verbal imagery of the turbulent caged bird and snared prey with the final stage picture:

Stage Images and the 'National Argument'

> King, she is dead; but lay no hand upon her.
> What's this but empty cage and tangled wire,
> Now the bird's gone? (202)

When *Deirdre* reached final version through performance and revision, the Abbey Theatre had weathered many disputes over its depiction of Irish life. The riots attending performances of Yeats's *Countess Cathleen* and Synge's *Playboy of the Western World* are well known, and Lady Gregory summarised the conflict in *The Image* (1909), a play in which Irish villagers try in vain to design the statue of an ideal man:

> Brian Hosty's 'Image' was his native, passionately loved province of Connacht; but he boasted of it to some who could see its thorns and thistles with passionateless eyes, looking over the mering wall. Mrs. Coppinger had her mind set upon America as a place where the joy of life would reach its summit, but that hope is clouded by the derision of one who has been there, and seen but the ugliness about him. Costello thought of an earth all peace, but when he spoke of peace 'they made themselves ready for war'. Thomas Coppinger dreamed of a great monument he would make to some great man, and old Peggy of one made beautiful through long memory and death; and Malachi of one who was beyond and above earthly life. And each of these images crumbled at the touch of reality, like a wick that has escaped the flame, and is touched by common air.[28]

The epigrams to Yeats's *Responsibilities* (1914), a collection of poems written during the early Abbey years, recalled the same dispute: 'In dreams begins responsibility.' In a note to *The Image*, Lady Gregory praised Yeats's work in bringing the heroic ideal to the Irish stage:

> If the dreamer had never tried to tell the dream that had come across him, even though 'to betray his secret to the multitude' must shatter his own perfect vision, the world would grow clogged and dull with the weight of flesh and of clay. And so we must say 'God love you' to the Image-makers, for we do not live by the shining of those scattered fragments of their dream?[29]

Yeats's plan for the Abbey was increasingly at odds with the company itself. His proposal that the Abbey produce classical plays in the manner of a European repertory company was fiercely opposed by Synge and Lady Gregory, who insisted that the Abbey remain a national theatre. The Fay brothers, on the other hand, wanted an actors' theatre without the control of the directors; they finally left in 1907.[30] The following year

Players and Painted Stage

Miss Annie Horniman ended her financial support, urging Yeats to join her new Manchester Gaiety Theatre. Though he refused, Yeats began to look for new ways of carrying out the plans he had announced two years earlier in *The Arrow*:

We are now fairly satisfied with the representation of peasant life, and we can afford to give the greater part of our attention to other expressions of our art and of our life. Our romantic work and poetical work once reasonably good, we can, if but the dramatist arrive, take up the life of our drawing-rooms, and see if there is something characteristic there, something which our nationality may enable us to express better than others, and so create plays of that life and means to play them as beautiful as a play of Hauptmann's or of Ibsen's upon the German or the Scandinavian stage.[31]

The Abbey had not taken this path. Its peasant plays remained the best expression of its writers and actors. Yeats kept at work, though, determined to make the Abbey self-supporting. 'If at all possible,' he wrote in 1909, 'I will keep at the Theatre till I have seen produced a mass of fine work.'[32] By that time Yeats had a new plan for the Abbey — a second company to develop a more formal style of acting and production, and the collaboration of his friend Gordon Craig.

II
Dialogue into Movement: W. B. Yeats's Theatre Collaboration with Gordon Craig

'I have done nothing but theatre for months,' Yeats wrote to his father in 1912.[1] After Synge's death three years earlier, Yeats's responsibilities at the Abbey Theatre had greatly increased. He had even taken on its financial support, lecturing in England to raise funds for the theatre's maintenance. In the midst of this business, he renewed an old friendship with Gordon Craig that not only benefitted the Abbey but affected the whole of Yeats's own drama. His decision to revise some early plays dating from 1910 to 1913 was prompted by the chance to restage them in Craig's new scenery, and this use of stage space anticipated Yeats's adaptations, several years later, of the Japanese Noh drama.

The important years of Yeats's and Craig's collaboration were 1909 to 1912, years of the debut of Craig's scenery at the Abbey Theatre, revivals of *The Land of Heart's Desire, The Countess Cathleen,* and *The Hour-Glass,* and early drafts of *The Player Queen.* The friendship had begun earlier, in the days of the Irish Literary Theatre. Yeats saw Craig's first production in 1901 and realized immediately that it was the style of theatre he wanted. As he wrote to Craig, 'I thought your scenery to "Aeneas and Dido" the only good scenery I ever saw. You have created a new art. I have written to Frank Harris to ask him to let me do an article on the subject in his new paper "The Saturday Review".'[2] Yeats's interest in Craig's early productions for the Purcell Operatic Society was partly practical. There was no need for costly, elaborate scenery, and, as Yeats confided to Lady Gregory, a stolen glimpse backstage had given him ideas for inexpensive staging and costumes at the

Abbey.³ 'Illusion,' Yeats insisted,'... is impossible, and should not be attempted.'⁴ (See Plate 2.) Moreover, Craig's early productions showed him how to alter the stage space. By means of lighting, draped ribbons could become a tent; tied grey curtains, the columns of a grand interior. An actor, freed from the blocking demand by footlights, could move into new spaces on a stage lit by back and side lighting. Stage space, then, offered the actor new possibilities for movement. In Yeats's words,

> The primary value of Mr. Craig's invention is that it enables one to use light in a more natural and more beautiful way than ever before. We get rid of all the top hamper of the stage, all the hanging ropes and scenes which prevent the free play of light. It is now possible to substitute in the shading of one scene real light and shadow for painted light and shadow.... One enters into a world of decorative effect which gives the actor a renewed importance.[5]

This kind of theatre — where form is content, in Kenneth Burke's phrase — especially caught Yeats's imagination. He had continually placed emphasis on form in his own work. 'A beautiful soul,' Yeats paraphrased Spenser, 'makes for itself a beautiful body.'[6] He suggested in 'Edmund Spenser' (1902) that the original Irishman 'spoke a language even in which it was all but impossible to think an abstract thought.'[7] For the same reason he praised Lady Gregory's *Cuchulain of Muirthemne* (1902): 'I know of no language to write about Ireland in but raw modern English; but now Lady Gregory has discovered a speech as beautiful as that of Morris, and a living speech into the bargain.'[8] Craig's scenic art, then, seemed to Yeats a form inseparable from an actor's language and movement: 'Decorative scene-painting would be ... as inseparable from the movements as from the robes of the players and from the falling of the light; and ... it would mingle with the tones of the voices and with the sentiment of the play, without overwhelming them under an alien interest.'[9] 'The truth is,' he announced in 1901, 'that the Irish people are at the precise stage of their history when imagination, shaped by many stirring events, desires dramatic expression.'[10] His inspired description of Merrie Englishmen reads both as a type for modern Irishmen and as an ideal for a theatre that could teach Ireland a new image of oneself: 'Men still wept when they were moved, still dressed themselves in joyous colours, and spoke with many gestures.'[11] He fashioned Spenser into the type of artist who 'seemed always to feel through the eyes, imagining everything in pictures,'[12] but he took for his own model the Elizabethan dramatists whose subject 'was always the soul, the whimsical, self-awakening, self-exciting, self-appeasing soul. They celebrated its heroical, passionate will going by its own path to immortal and invisible things.'[13] Nietzsche's terms begin to appear in this essay, enforcing the argument for a theatre based not on pictures but on a space inseparable from the actor, a theatre not of the eye but of the body: 'In Ireland, where the tide of life is rising, we turn, not to picture-making, but to the imagination of personality — to drama, gesture.'[14]

Craig's productions, then, gave direction to Yeats's early work at the Abbey. In 1902, Yeats encouraged the Abbey actor Frank Fay to keep at his 'acting of verse' because he himself had been 'in the same state about scenery that I am now in about acting. I knew the right principles but I did not know the right practice because I had never seen it. I have now however learnt a great deal from Gordon Craig.'[15] In his lecture 'The Reform of the Theatre' (1911), Yeats illustrated the new stage design on a small model stage Craig had made for him.[16] Edith Craig took Yeats backstage during her brother's production of Housman's *Bethlehem* (1902). As Yeats recounted to Lady Gregory, 'I have learned a great deal about the staging of plays from 'the nativity', indeed I have learned more than Craig likes. His sister has helped me, bringing me to where I could see the way the lights were worked. He was indignant — there was quite an amusing scene. I have seen all the costumes too.'[17] The three of them, Yeats, Craig and Craig's sister, planned several joint productions. Edith Craig persuaded the Stage Society to produce Yeats's play, *Where There Is Nothing*, though Craig too wanted 'to produce it with elaborate scenery instead of the Maeterlinck which they had asked him to do.'[18] Two plans for Yeats's plays, as we shall see, were eventually accomplished at the Abbey. One was a production of *The Hour-Glass*, which, in scenario form, 'greatly delighted' Craig.[19] But the grandest scheme of those early years was a production that would have combined the verse-speaking and stage design Yeats wanted: 'Sturge Moore was round with me last night and he made to

Gordon Craig (through a friend of Craig's that was there) an offer on Ricketts' behalf. He proposed that Ricketts should raise nearly £600 which should be used by Craig to stage my *Countess Cathleen*. All the speaking of verse to be left entirely in the hands of Sturge Moore and of course the author.'[20]

Yeats thought such a production would 'enormously strengthen' his position, but he soon realised that Craig's intentions differed in principle from his own. Craig wanted a drama composed of movement and light, the kind of drama later developed by Diaghilev's Russian Ballet.[21] Yeats was concerned more with the primacy of language than with movement. Though he often praised Craig for creating 'an ideal country where everything was possible,' his own ideal theatre included 'speaking in verse, or speaking to music.'[22] Craig's scenery, Yeats wrote to Lady Gregory after a performance of *The Vikings* (1903), 'is amazing but rather distracts one's thought from the words.'[23] He invited Florence Farr to Dublin to see his own scenery for the 1905 production of *The Shadowy Waters*: 'You will I think prefer it to Craig. It is more noble and simple.'[24] He described this production in Craig's terms — 'What I have done is but a form and colour in an elaborate composition' — though he intended these stage conventions to frame a 'speech even more important than gesture upon the stage.'[25] Having followed Florence Farr's London performances in Greek tragedies, Yeats placed his own notion of theatre in that tradition. Classical Greek acting had been great, he claimed, 'because it did all but everything with the voice.' The new style of theatre would combine Craig's art with his own: 'Modern acting may be great when it does everything with voice and movement.'[26] Not until his later collaboration with Craig was Yeats able to present on stage a combination of language and movement that approached his early ideal.

'He has altered his verse and his drama to fit the stage. He has done wrong.'[27] This pronouncement was part of Craig's review of Yeats's *Plays for an Irish Theatre* (1911). By the time the review appeared, Yeats was again altering his drama to fit a stage. The Abbey's small proscenium stage had been transformed by Craig's new scenery for the January 1911 production of Lady Gregory's *The Deliverer* and Yeats's *The Hour-Glass*.[28] Craig's scenery did more than transform the Abbey: it

Dialogue into Movement

greatly affected Yeats's revisions and subsequent work. To follow those revisions, two things should be kept in mind — Craig's original intentions for new stage scenery, and his practical solution used at the Abbey.

Early in 1907, Craig completed the design for his ideal stage set. (See Plates 3a and 3b.) He wanted 'a "*scene*" so mobile, which (within rules) might move in all directions — tempos — in all things under the control of the one who could dream how to move its parts to produce "*movements*". He designed a 'pliable floor' divided into a grid of squares, with cubes rising from each square. There would also be a 'roof composed of the same shapes as the floor — suspended cubes, each cube exactly covering (and meeting when lowered) each square on the floor.'[29] By means of a remote control instrument, he would control the lighting and movement of these cubes, composing performances of movement. To illustrate such a performance, he made a series of wood engravings (Plate 4), each illustrating a moment of 'arrested motion'.[30] When he established a theatre school in Florence, he experimented with more practical solutions for small theatres not equipped with hydraulic systems. For those theatres, he devised hinged screens that could be folded to form cubes, expanded into larger shapes, or even moved about slowly during performance.[31] He built a model (Plate 5) to practise with lighting and screens.

It was a sketch of his model that reanimated Yeats's interest in his and Craig's early plans for productions. In London during January 1910, Craig dined with Yeats, sketching and explaining his invention. The following day Yeats wrote to Lady Gregory, 'I am to see his model .... I think I shall, if it seems right, order one for us.' Yeats saw that the invention would radically alter the problems of dramatic construction posed by the Abbey stage. 'I now think,' he continued, '... that a certain modification will give us an entirely adequate open air scene. That we shall have a means of staging everything that is not naturalistic, and that out of his invention may grow a completely new method even for our naturalistic plays. I think we could get rid of side scenes even for naturalistic plays.'[32] Craig, anxious that his invention be used correctly, was a stern bargainer. Yeats was discouraged from using the scenery for a proposed production of *Oedipus Rex*: 'He wants us to play about with his model first and master its effects.'³³ The firmest part of the bargain, though, was no obstacle for Yeats: 'If we accept the invention I must agree, he says, to use it for all my poetical work in the future. I would gladly agree.'³⁴ And so Craig's screens were adopted by the Abbey Theatre. The next few seasons were filled with experiment and revision, until the restrictions of the war sent Yeats's players to the music halls for a living.³⁵ In the meantime, Yeats had committed not only the Abbey to Craig's style of theatre. On 24 November 1910, he wrote to his father, 'I shall get all my plays into the Craig scene.'³⁶

The plays Yeats first put into Craig's scenery were not new ones. Initially he took three old plays, *The Land of Heart's Desire, The Countess Cathleen*, and *The Hour-Glass*, and produced them in the new scenery (1911) before rewriting them. The new versions were produced the following year.³⁷ Several projects led to Yeats's selection of these three plays. *The Land of Heart's Desire* had long been the most popular of his plays for amateur groups, and he wanted to bring it closer to contemporary stage techniques.³⁸ *The Countess Cathleen*, perhaps his favourite play, and *The Hour-Glass* were both plays he and Craig once planned to produce. Yeats may also have wanted to rework these plays because of his current studies. 'I have been lecturing on the Other World,' he wrote to his father in 1912, 'and am now writing the lecture as an introduction to Lady Gregory's big book of Fairy Belief. I think I have made the first philosophic generalization that has been made from the facts of spiritism and the facts of folklore in combination.'³⁹ Yeats considered *The Land of Heart's Desire* and *The Countess Cathleen* as miracle plays, 'by which he meant plays not necessarily Christian but manifesting in one way or another the existence of an invisible world.'⁴⁰ *The Hour-Glass* — originally called a morality play — was in Yeats's words 'a parable of the conscious and the subconscious life.'⁴¹ Yeats made *The Hour-Glass* into one of the best of his early one-act plays, and it deserves close attention. First, though, a consideration of revisions in the other two plays will illustrate changes in stage space and language that led to the new version of *The Hour-Glass*.

The Land of Heart's Desire was the least revised of the plays.

Dialogue into Movement

Though Yeats had become more skilled in dialogue construction, the characters remain the embodiment of lyric voices in the early poems, especially 'The Stolen Child,' 'The Ballad of Father Hart,' and 'The Song of the Old Mother.'[42] The play depicts the choice between the visible and invisible worlds, the daily round of Christian duties and the life of the Faery. The young wife Mary chooses the Faery way, against the persuasions of her husband's parents and a superstitious but well-meaning priest. Her husband, 'too full of drowsy love,' sighs that he cannot give her both choices:

> Would that the world were mine to give it you,
> And not its quiet hearths alone, but even
> All that bewilderment of light and freedom,
> If you would have it. (62)

The 1912 revision presents this choice — between Mary's book or the mother's hearth, the world of poetry and the Faery or the weariness of the "four tongues' — in the stage setting.

The original stage directions called for a kitchen room, with everyone except the Faery Child on stage the entire time. All argument about the two choices was in the dialogue. In the new version, Yeats set the play in the kind of scenery he had used for *Deirdre*: a room opening to trees and beyond, using Craig's lighting, to a 'vague, mysterious world.'[43] This new stage space gives greater coherence to metaphors in the dialogue. Take, for instance, the love scene between Mary and Shawn, which, like the chess scene in *Deirdre*, combines the words with the stage set. In the new scenery, the hearth and family are to the right, Mary's bench and book of poetry to the left, and beyond, the mysterious wood with its silver light. This setting reinforces the verse:

> Mary. Oh, you are the great door-post of this house,
> And I the branch of blessed quicken wood,
> And if I could I'd hang upon the post
> Till I had brought good luck into the house. (61-62)

Mary's attentions are fixed on the faery world outside, yet she can still imagine a sort of domesticity. Her speech bears more relation to her actions than the original lines:

> O, you are the great door-post of this house,
> And I the red nasturtium climbing up.[44]

Yeats revised towards a language that not only acts with the stage space, but grows from the movement within it. Mary's 'blessed quicken wood' recalls her placing a bough of quicken wood upon the doorpost to keep out the Faeries. In the original version, she had strewn primroses before the door. Now, the branch is quickly removed by a Faery Child from the "vague, mysterious world." By using the set together with the words and actions of the players, Yeats has constructed the whole of Mary's choice. In this way, her final words to the Faery Child — 'I will go with you' — conclude an action that began in the stage movement.

Yeats's revision of *The Countess Cathleen* was more extensive than that of *The Land of Heart's Desire*. With a different setting, he staged it as it had first appeared — as a series of pictures. Before the first production in May 1899, the play had been performed as a sequence of "living pictures," each a different episode in the play.[45] These *tableaux vivants* and the following production were disappointing, for Yeats had not yet learned how to make 'scenery and costumes which will draw little attention to themselves and cost little money.'[46] That disappointment, he recalled after revising the play for Craig's scenery, had let to another type of drama: 'It was, indeed, the first performance of "The Countess Cathleen," when our stage-pictures were made out of poor conventional scenery and hired costumes, that set me writing plays where all would depend upon the player.'[47]

Yeats extensively reworked Scene II of *The Countess Cathleen*, a depiction of Cathleen's choice from which the action develops. As in *The Land of Heart's Desire*, Yeats reconstructed the choice by coordinating language and movement. In the first version, Scene II is set in the great hall of Cathleen's home, where she returns for refuge from famine. The backcloth is a tapestry 'representing the loves and wars and huntings of the Fenian and Red Branch warriors,'[48] the idealized figures dominating the entire scene. The foster mother Oona uses the tapestry to comfort Cathleen, suggesting that she

... make a soft cradle of old tales,
And songs, and music ...[49]

The world of legend can suffice as a refuge. Though Cathleen

Dialogue into Movement

eventually abandons that refuge to give her riches to the peasants, the tapestry belittles her choice. When Yeats described two kinds of poetry — the creation of pictures and the imagination of personality — he wrote that 'pictures make us sorrowful. We share the poet's separation from what he describes. It is life in the mirror.'[50] For all her choosing, Cathleen in the early version is sorrowful. The tapestry remains a reminder not of what she chose, but of what she deserted.

There is no tapestry in the 1912 version. The second scene is now set in a 'wood with perhaps distant view of turreted house at one side, but all in flat colour, without light and shade and against a diapered or gold background.' The poet and lover Aleel has been added, and together with Oona he represents retreat; she offers the comforts of the hearth, he the refuge of legend:

> I thought to have kept her from remembering
> The evil of the times for full ten minutes (19)

The three characters now move within a space, no longer dominated by the tapestry picture, which takes its meaning from their speech and movement. Cathleen enters:

> Surely this leafy corner, where one smells
> The wild bee's honey, has a story too? (17)

Oona tries to point out the house, the end of her journey, but Cathleen's thoughts are with Aleel. His words create the space.

> A man, they say,
> Loved Maeve the Queen of all the invisible host,
> And died of his love nine centuries ago.
> And now, when the moon's riding at the full,
> She leaves her dancers lonely and lies there
> Upon that level place, and for three days
> Stretches and sighs and wets her long pale cheeks. (17)

Cathleen and Aleel take up the story of the two legendary lovers, but Oona's insistence — 'There is your own house, lady' — ends the tale. It is not only the telling that is interrupted as if the reciting of an old tale were a gesture towards the figures in a tapestry. Cathleen and Aleel had discovered in the story a situation similar to their own. The tale had served to focus their own thoughts: might the distracted Cathleen, like Queen Maeve, forget her lover?

> But there is nothing that will stop in their heads,
> They've such poor memories, though they weep for it.
> O yes, they weep; that's when the moon is full. (18)

Aleel is angered by Oona's interruption, for the tale might have ended with a better image for the lovers:

> A curse upon it for a meddlesome house!
> Had it but stayed away I would have known
> What Queen Maeve thinks on when the moon is pinched. (18)

The two following episodes — the arrival of the Steward and then Teig and Shemus — are greatly compressed from earlier versions. With a minimum of explanation, the stage space could become the Steward's approach to the house or, for Teig and Shemus, part of the neighbourhood path. By the end of the scene, the dialogue has added a further meaning to the stage space. Cathleen makes her choice. No longer is she searching for a private refuge, a house to keep out the troubles:

> Come, follow me, for the earth burns my feet
> Till I have changed my house to such a refuge
> That the old and ailing, and all weak of heart,
> May escape from beak and claw; all, all, shall come
> Till the walls burst and the roof fall on us.
> From this day out I have nothing of my own. (24)

When Yeats finished the 1912 version of *The Land of Heart's Desire* and *The Countess Cathleen*, he explained what had guided his revision: 'In their new shape — and each play has been twice played during the winter — they have given me some pleasure, and are, I think, easier to play effectively than my later plays, depending less upon the players and more upon the producer, both having been imagined more for variety of stage-picture than variety of mood in the player.'[51] *The Countess Cathleen* remains a construction 'devised episode by episode'.[52] Yeats's revisions and the threading of Aleel's story through the original plot explain much of its episodic nature. It may also be true that the initial performance of the play as a sequence of 'living pictures' interfered with the development of a strong and simple plot. Yeats's early Abbey plays — *The King's Threshold, Deirdre,* and *The Shadowy Waters* — were

Dialogue into Movement

constructed as single episodes, a method Yeats perfected in the dance plays. Professor Ure suggests that 'one method of distinguishing his more successful plays from the others is to observe that in them the story is *about* the place, or, to put it another way, that the characters have to come to just this place, and no other anywhere in the world, so that this story may happen.'[53] The single episode of *The Hour-Glass*, set within Gordon Craig's new scenery, was the most important of Yeats's 1912 revisions.

The new version of *The Hour-Glass* represents most clearly Yeats's new style of theatre in which dialogue is enacted in performance. The original play was based on Lady Wilde's story 'The Priest's Soul,' and Yeat's revisions gave it as varied a history as *The Countess Cathleen*.[54] From the time he first read the scenario to Craig in 1902 until the play was produced in Craig's scenery in 1912 and published the following year in *The Mask*, *The Hour-Glass* changed not only from one style of theatre to another but from one style of language to another. There is the early verse, in the Angel's speech:

> You have to die because no soul has passed
> The heavenly threshold since you have opened school,
> But grass grows there, and rust upon the hinge;
> And they are lonely that must keep the watch.[55]   (308)

Here is the pre-Raphaelite imagery, the poetry of picture-making, that Yeats came to consider a weakness in his verse. Translated into stage movement, this is Oona in *The Countess Cathleen* pointing to the tapestry of heroes. The early prose passages work in the same way. There is no movement of thought enacted in the words. The prose, with its even rhythms and repetitive logic merely refers:

> Wise Man. Though they call him Teigue the Fool, he is not more foolish than everybody used to be, with their dreams and their preachings and their three worlds; but I have overthrown their three worlds with the seven sciences. [*He touches the books with his hands.*] With Philosophy that was made from the lonely star, I have taught them to forget Theology; with Architecture, I have hidden the ramparts of their cloudy Heaven; with Music ...[56]

'With Music, ... with Arithmetic ... Rhetoric and Dialectic ...': neither the imagery nor the rhythm in such language can embody a moment of changing perception, of dramatic movement.

Despite the early prose, there is the verse that, in T. R. Henn's words, anticipates 'the thought of the "irrational force" in "The Second Coming", the dance of agony and frenzy in "Byzantium".'[57] The imagery suggests the movement of perception:

> Reason is growing dim;
> A moment more, and Frenzy will beat his drum
> And laugh aloud and scream;
> And I must dance in the dream.
> No, no, but it is like a hawk, a hawk of the air,
> It has swooped down — and this swoop makes the third —
> And what can I, but tremble like a bird? (303)

The rhythm is uneven, creating the tight, labouring breath of fear. The images are spatial: 'dance,' 'swoop,' 'tremble.' The language is spatial in another sense too. As Yeats wrote in 'Discoveries,' the greatest art expresses moods that are a 'conflagration of all the energies of active life,' the energy of 'the whole man.'[58] In dramatic art, this is the energy displayed in an actor's voice and movement. When Yeats revised *The Hour-Glass*, the verse reflected the kind of movement made possible by the new stage space.

Gordon Craig's stage setting was a catalyst for the new revision. Yeats praised Craig's designs for the production in November 1912. They 'helped me wonderfully, and I think I have banished platitude from the "Hour-Glass" ...'[59] Craig's scenery was quite different from the symmetrical set of the original production in 1903 (Plate 6), the Wise Man's study with back and side doors, adorned with an astronomical globe, a map, and musical instruments. 'The master's desk,' Yeats was advised, 'is to stand bang in the centre of the stage but near the back wall, leaving only room for his stool behind it.'[60] Such emphasis on the Wise Man's learning had the same effect as the overpowering tapestry in *The Countess Cathleen*. Yeats later regretted the constant visual focus: 'I have found that the brown back of a chair during the performance of *The Hour-Glass* annoyed me beyond words.'[61]

In Craig's new design (see Plates 7 and 9) the Wise Man's study is only part of the set. The desk, now in profile, is in an alcove at the right front corner, in shadow. From the study, a corridor of screens curves round to the left, disappearing back centre stage into light. This arrangement suggests that the Wise Man's place is at one point of a circular pathway, that his domain of learning is at the dark end of a path moving towards light. The set anticipates the circling, gyring, and lunar phases of Yeats's later imagery, the kind of movement Yeats already considered symbolic: 'Motions are also symbolic ... Going and returning are the typical eternal motions, they characterize the visionary forms of eternal life. They belong to *up and down*, to *in and out*.'[62]

In addition to a stage set composed of opposites — light, shadow, circle, square — Craig helped shape the opposition between the Fool and the Wise Man through his mask designs. During rehearsal for the new production in January 1911, Yeats wrote to Lady Gregory that he was 'very much excited by the thought of putting the fool into a mask and rather amused at the idea of an angel in a golden domino.... Craig evidently wants to keep what is superhuman from being inhuman.'[63] Craig had included many drawings and articles on the art of the mask in his theatre journal *The Mask*. In his view, masks were 'the only right medium of portraying the expressions of the soul as shown through the expressions of the face.'[64] 'The advantage of a mask over a face is that it is always repeating unerringly the poetic fancy.... Durability was the dominant idea in Egyptian art. The theatre must learn that lesson.... Let us again cover the actor's face with a mask in order that his expression — the visualized expression of the Poetic spirit — shall be everlasting.'[65] Yeats hoped the Abbey would be 'the first modern theatre to use the mask.' He saw in Craig's 'visualized Poetic spirit' a way of altering not only *The Hour-Glass*: 'If the masks work right I would put the fool and the blind man in *Baile's Strand* into masks.'[66] After the 1911 revival he began revising both plays. 'If you will read my play *Baile's Strand* in the book I send you,' he wrote to Craig, 'I'd like to know if you think that the fool and the blind man ought to wear a mask.'[67] A month later Craig sent him the design. (See Plates 8 and 10.)

The coincidence of revising and redesigning both plays left its mark on *The Hour-Glass*. In *On Baile's Strand*, the conflict between Cuchulain and Cuchubar is the same as that between the Fool and the Blind Man. As Yeats remarked, Cuchulain 'is the fool — wandering, passive, houseless and almost loveless. Concobhar is reason that is blind because it can only reason because it is cold. Are they not the cold moon and the hot sun?'[68] A similar pattern appears in the verse revision of *The Hour-Glass*. No longer does the Wise Man simply interview the Fool. Now the two characters act out complementary roles, one with words, one with movement. As the Fool remarks at the end, 'You and I, we are the two fools, we know everything but we will not speak.'

In explaining the verse revision, Yeats stressed the importance of mask and movement. 'An action on the stage,' he noted in his preface to the version printed in *The Mask* (1913), 'is so much stronger than a word that when the Wise Man abused himself before the Fool I was ashamed.'[69] He had special problems with the Wise Man, a type of character passionate only in argument:[70] 'Those learned men who are a terror to children and an ignominious sight in lovers' eyes, all those butts of a traditional humour where there is something of the wisdom of peasants, are mathematicians, theologians, lawyers, men of science of various kinds. They have followed some abstract reverie, which stirs the brain only.'[71] Yeats's revisions of the dialogue emphasise the limits of the Wise Man's wisdom. In the 1922 verse version, the addition of 'medieval Latin' passages isolated more clearly the mode of argument of the Wise Man and his pupils from the rest of the dialogue.[72] The main revision of the Wise Man lies not in the dialogue alone, but in the relation between his words and the Fool's mimes. 'I even doubt,' Yeats wrote, 'if any play had ever a great popularity that did not use, or seem to use, the bodily energies of its principal actor to the full.'[73] In *The Hour-Glass*, the bodily energies are those of the Fool who mimes the Wise Man's learning in such a way that his discoveries are presented as much in movement as in dialogue.

The first of these changes occurs in the opening scene. No longer is the audience presented with the Wise Man alone. Instead, his pupils appear before the curtain to choose a subject for the day's lesson. This revision 'allows us to come to know the protagonist, at first, through the remarks and

Dialogue into Movement

comments made by his pupils. The confusion and doubt in which the Pupils find themselves lead to the atmosphere of doubt and spiritual frustration which has been the achievement of the Wise Man.'[74] The pupils' uncertainty is interrupted by the Fool:

> Fool. Give me a penny.
>
> Second Pupil. Let us choose a subject by chance. Here is his big book. Let us turn over the pages slowly. Let one of us put down his finger without looking. The passage his finger lights on will be the subject for the lesson.
>
> Fool. Give me a penny. (300)

From his first entrance the Fool mimes the others on stage. The pupils' choice, hardly a considered decision, is left to chance; poking for snippets of a text differs little from collecting the odd penny. This similarity is expressed in the Fool's mime, which ends the scene:

> Fourth Pupil. Down on your knees. Hunch up your back. Spread your arms out now, and look like a golden eagle in a church. Keep still, keep still. (300)

No supporting lectern, no open book, and as the Fool plays at holding up the book, the pupils play at choosing a lesson from it.

> First Pupil. There, I have chosen. Fool, keep still — and if what's wise is strange and sounds like nonsense, we've made a good choice. (300)

The curtain opens, revealing the Wise Man at his corner desk. A pupil reads him the text:

> 'There are two living countries, one visible and one invisible, and when it is summer there, it is winter here, and when it is November with us, it is lambing-time there.' (301)

The Wise Man frantically begins the lesson, recognising in the passage the same irrationality that guided the pupils' choosing. The troublesome passage, one student tries to explain, was written by a beggar upon the walls of Babylon, Yeats's city of mathematical abstraction.[75] They ask their own beggar for an interpretation, but the Fool does not answer in the Wise Man's terms:

> To be sure — everybody knows, everybody in the world knows, when it is spring with us, the trees are withering there, when it is summer with us, the snow is falling there, and have I not myself heard the lambs that are there all bleating on a cold November day — to be sure, does not everybody with an intellect know that? And maybe when it's night with us, it is day with them, for many a time I have seen the roads lighted before me.[76]
>
> (302)

The Fool is also 'Teigue,' the traditional name for a stage Irishman. In the original production, Yeats followed the traditional type even in Teigue's costume. 'Let the fool's wig,' he had written to Frank Fay who was rehearsing the part, '... be red and matted.'[77] The Wise Man translates the Fool's foolishness into the language of an educated scholar — he speaks of human faculties, worldly kingdoms and spiritual kingdoms. His pupils, not yet having mastered their lessons, change his terms back into the Fool's own imagery:

> If he [the beggar of Babylon] meant all that, I will take an oath that he was spindle-shanked, and cross-eyed, and had a lousy itching shoulder, and that his heart was crosser than his eyes, and that he wrote it out of malice.[78]
>
> (302)

The Wise Man's language soon gives way to the verse quoted earlier, to frantic rhythm and images of violent bodily movement.

> Reason is growing dim;
> A moment more and Frenzy will beat his drum
> And laugh aloud and scream;
> And I must dance in the dream. (303)

His words point beyond the character to the stage space. Reason grows dim; his study remains in shadow, while his pupils disappear down a corridor of light. For the moment, the Wise Man insists that 'whole wisdom' is 'to see rightly whatever the dream' because 'everybody is a fool when he is asleep and dreaming.' Yeats makes full use of the stage in this notion of seeing.

This is the classical image, as in Sophocles' *Oedipus Rex*, which Yeats had hoped to produce in 1910[79]; sight is blindness, insight is seeing into what has been invisible. Yeats joins this metaphor with his own imagery of sunlight and moonlight. Sleep, dreams, the subjective 'lunar' insights, at first appear suspect. 'There's nothing,' the Wise Man declares, 'but what men can see when they are awake,' but soon doubts whether his pupils really share his world of learning. They merely give him back his own words, as the Fool mimes his speech:

> Well, there are your four pennies — Fool, you are called,
> And all day long they cry, 'Come hither, Fool'.
> 							*[The Fool goes close to him.*
> Or else it's 'Fool, be gone'.
> 							*[The Fool goes further off.*
> Or, 'Fool, stand there'.
> 							*[The Fool straightens himself up.*
> Or, 'Fool, go sit in the corner'.
> 							*[The Fool sits in the corner.*
>   And all the while
> What were they all but fools before I came?
> What are they now but mirrors that seem men
> Because of my image? Fool, hold up your head.
> 							*[The Fool does so.* (307)

When the Fool claims he has been followed by an angel, the Wise Man muses on the foolish tale of spirits who

> Would solidly out-stare
> The steadiest eyes with their unnatural eyes,
> Aye, on a man's own floor. (307)

An Angel enters,[80] and for a moment the stage is filled with three kinds of seeing. The Angel, with the 'unnatural eyes' of Craig's mask, is seen at once by the Fool. He had said he could catch sight of angels if he was so quiet 'that there is not a thought in One's head.' The Wise Man is still wrapped in his own thoughts,

> ... haunted by the notion
> That there's a crisis of the spirit wherein
> We get new sight (308)

When the Fool calls for quiet, the Wise Man turns to see the Angel.

Yeats continued to revise the dialogue at this point to get the words in line with the stage movement. The 1911 prose version contained these lines:

> Wise Man. I have denied and taught the like to others.

> Believing nothing but what sense has taught,
> And the mind's abstract.
>
> Angel. It is too late for pardon.
>
> Wise Man. Had I but seen your face as now I see it...[81]

In the verse version printed in *Responsibilities* (1914), the emphasis has been changed from recollection — 'what sense had taught' — to the immediate act of seeing:

> Wise Man. I have denied and taught the like to others.
> But how could I believe before my sight
> Had come to me?
>
> Angel.   It is too late for pardon.
>
> Wise Man. Had I but met your gaze as now I meet it...   (309)

The Wise Man learns he is to die within the hour. Like the souls in Dante's *Inferno*, he will take the shape of his learned language:

> Hell is the place of those who have denied;
> They find there what they planted and what dug,
> A Lake of Spaces, and a Wood of Nothing,
> And wander there and drift, and never cease
> Wailing for substance.   (309)

The Wise Man's development has been described as a rejection of reason and renunciation of self in order to rediscover 'the mood by which truth is perceived and the processes by which the knowledge of it could have grown.'[82] The discovery of the limits of his language is also a discovery of his resemblance to the Fool. The Angel's comments link the two characters. The Wise Man can be spared, he explains, only if he can find a believer,

> One fish to lie and spawn among the stones
> Till the great Fisher's net is full again   (310)

The Fool appears, with the long pair of shears. (See Plate 11.) Earlier, when the Wise Man asked about the shears, the Fool explained:

> ...Every day men go out
> dressed in black and spread great black nets
> over the hills, great black nets.
>
> Wise Man. A strange place to fish in.

> Fool. They spread them out on the hills that they may catch the feet of the angels; but every morning, just before dawn, I go out and cut the nets with the shears and the angels fly away.
>
> (305)

Though the Wise Man scoffs at the tale, he soon finds it a curious version of the effect of his own learning. The great Fisher's net, the Angel explains, has been empty since he opened school. The 1911 prose version makes explicit the connection between the Fool and the great Fisher:

> Fisherman lets me sleep among the nets in his loft in the winter-time because he says I bring him luck...[83]

In subsequent versions, 'Fisherman' becomes 'fishermen,' perhaps because the new costume made such lines redundant.

The analogy between the Wise Man emptying the Fisher's net and the Fool freeing angels from men's nets works in several ways. The emptying of nets is similar to the Fool's mime of the Wise Man's words as well as his mime of the pupils' lectern. Wisdom, in the familiar paradox, appears foolish. The resemblance has another effect, for the Fool's wisdom is wisdom of the body. He claims his presence brings luck to fishermen, and he can see the Angel before the Wise Man does. In this way, what has been the Fool's nonsense — his story of the nets — is now the Wise Man's freedom. A story, an image, has revealed his preoccupation better than all his argument.

To be saved, the Wise Man must find one believer, and once again the Fool mimes the action. Clutching his large money bag (Plate 11), the Fool refuses to admit any belief:

> I will not speak. I will not tell you what is in my mind. I will not tell you what is in my bag. You might steal away my thoughts.[84]
>
> (322)

In the prose version, a pupil asks, 'Teigue, will you give us your pennies if we teach you lessons?' And again, Wise Man sees his own desire. Collecting words — and it is a confession of belief he needs, not just a believer — is like saving up pennies. Now he needs no words:

> The stream of the world has changed its course,
> And with the stream my thoughts have run
> Into some cloudy thunderous spring

> That is its mountain source —
> Aye, to some frenzy of the mind,
> For all that we have done's undone,
> Our speculation but as the wind. (323)

He bids the Fool be silent, and he dies.[85]

This final stage picture is part of Yeats's new dramatic style, representing a type of knowledge not depicted in the naturalistic social drama. 'Wisdom and beauty and power may sometimes,' he wrote, '... come to those who die every day they live, though their dying may not be like the dying Shakespeare spoke of.'[86] Gordon Craig dismissed realistic drama as 'inhuman' and wrote, in sympathy with Yeats, of a drama that could present that 'mysterious, joyous, and superbly complete life which is called Death.'[87] This is the death presented at the close of *The Hour-Glass*. On stage there is an angel, a fool and a dead man. 'The self,' Yeats believed, 'which is the foundation of our knowledge, is broken in pieces by foolishness.' Such foolishness 'may be a kind of death.'[88] The Angel carries away the butterfly soul of the Wise Man, and the Fool closes the curtain, inviting the audience to watch him:

> He is gone, he is gone, he is gone, but come
> in, everybody in the world, and look at me.
>   I hear the wind a-blow,
>   I hear the grass a-grow,
>   And all that I know, I know.
> But I will not speak, I will run away.
>   [*He goes out.*[89] (324)

This use of the lyric, similar to the song that ends *The Land of Heart's Desire*, is a technique Yeats developed in his dance plays. Here, the Fool — like the old hermit in 'The Three Hermits' — gives not an argument but a song for his thought. 'I had not learned what sweetness, what rhythmic movement,' Yeats wrote in 'Discoveries,' 'there is in those who have become the joy that is themselves.'[90] In the poem, two hermits argue while the third hermit,

> Giddy with his hundredth year,
> Sang unnoticed like a bird.

When Yeats wrote the poem in 1913, he was staying with Ezra Pound at Stone Cottage, Sussex. Their work on the Japanese

Dialogue into Movement

plays Pound was editing is part of the story of Yeats's own dance plays, a development of the work he had done with Gordon Craig. In *The Mask* Craig acknowledged his collaboration with Yeats: 'I have myself acted as a most willing aid in the interpretation of the drama of Yeats and it has been one of the special happinesses of my life to have been connected with his poetic dramas in Dublin... but only as a servant... seeing his as a 'brother art.'[91] Craig was more interested in a 'mimodrama' of mime and movement, though he admitted in *Towards a New Theatre* (1913) that 'My friend W. B. Yeats says that the scene is by no means disconnected with the art of poetry.'[92] Yeats's next drama was based on the Japanese Noh form, but his skill in fitting dialogue to movement was a skill he had learned from Craig. As he wrote to Craig in 1913, 'Your work is always a great inspiration to me. Indeed I cannot imagine myself writing any play for the stage now, which I did not write for your screens.'[93]

III
An Intimate Theatre: The Japanese Noh Drama and Yeats's Dance Plays

Gordon Craig's new scenery strengthened Yeats's adaptation of Irish stories for stage performance. In revisions of early plays and new work, Yeats clarified the theme by an increasingly visual presentation. This development was accompanied by a radical change in dialogue, in which the dense allusive language of *The Countess Cathleen, Deirdre*, and the early version of *The Hour-Glass* was replaced by a more direct and forceful speech. *The Green Helmet* (1910), based on an incident from the Cuchulain cycle and written in four-beat lines close to Irish speech rhythms, has been described as 'one of Yeats's complete dramatic successes; it has not any deliberateness, intentionalness, self-consciousness; it has spontaneity that goes well with high and heroic exploit. Indeed, the spirit of Irish heroic saga has never been better brought out than in this impetuous and humorous play.'[1] Yeats's work in consolidating scene and language in his own plays led in turn to a renewed interest in establishing a repertory company trained in verse-speaking and stylised movement. In September 1911, Yeats announced his plans for a second company to carry on the work of the Abbey Company during its first American tour. Addressing the audience after a performance of *Deirdre*, Yeats explained the purpose of the new 'school of dramatic art':

> We have placed at the head of it this autumn Mr. Nugent Monck, an Irishman of imagination and energy, who has learnt his art of the stage under Mr. Poel, of the Elizabethan Stage Society.... Our object is to train players to express the mind, and to copy the life of Ireland. Mr. Monck, with the help of his pupils, and probably some professional players, will give certain productions at the Abbey Theatre — perhaps a classical play, probably some

old interludes and mysteries, as well as reviving a play or two from our repertory. We hope that in the course of time we shall have trained in this manner a second company which will play at the Abbey when the main company is away, and we shall not greatly regret if we train also some rivals to ourselves.[2]

Under Nugent Monck's direction, the second company gave a number of performances in 1911 and 1912.[3] The Abbey stage was made level and extended by an apron stage and flight of steps, enabling the actors to move between the stage and the auditorium in productions of miracle plays.[4] Following this experimentation with earlier forms of drama and stage presentation, Yeats discovered the catalyst for his work with Gordon Craig and the Abbey's second company — the Japanese Noh plays.

Yeats was introduced to the plays in 1913 by Ezra Pound, who was preparing an edition of Ernest Fenollosa's important translations of the Noh.[5] While Yeats and Pound worked together at Stone Cottage during the winters of 1913, 1914 and 1915, Fenollosa's manuscripts became the centre of their discussion of poetry and drama. Though Yeats had seen illustrations of the Noh in the British Museum collection and in numerous issues of *The Mask*,[6] neither he nor Pound had seen the Noh plays performed. It was surely the incompleteness of his knowledge that allowed Yeats to draw so freely from the Fenollosa manuscript general principles that appeared to confirm his own work. Here at last was a form of 'intimate theatre'; masked actors, surrounded on three sides by the audience, could perform unencumbered by the separation between proscenium stage and stalls. In 'The Tragic Theatre,' published in *The Mask* in 1910, Yeats set his interest in lyric feeling against the emphasis on character and situation in naturalistic drama: 'In poetical drama there is, it is held, an antithesis between character and lyric poetry, for lyric poetry — however much it move you when read out of a book — can, as these critics think, but encumber the action. Yet when we go back a few centuries and enter the great periods of drama, character grows less and sometimes disappears, and there is much lyric feeling, and at times a lyric measure will be wrought into a dialogue, a flowing measure that had well befitted music, or that more lumbering one of the sonnet.'[7]

Players and Painted Stage

The Noh drama, through its combination of poetry, music and dance, embodied the same lyric feeling Yeats sought in his own work. Moreover, the coherent stage images of the Noh and brilliant presentation of traditional Japanese stories seemed to Yeats a model of his own plans for the Abbey. In his early theatre work, he had been interested in the effects of juxtaposed stage images and would have liked to see a complementary version of his play *The King's Threshold*: 'I took the plot of it from a Middle Irish story about the demands of the poets at the court of King Guaire, but twisted it about and revised its moral that the poet might have the best of it. One of my fellow-playwrights is going, I have hope, to take the other side and make a play that can be played after it, as in Greece the farce followed the tragedy.'[8] Early Abbey productions had shown Yeats the value of complementary stage images: 'I write of the tragic stories told over the fire by people who are in the comedies of my friends, and I never see my work played with theirs that I do not feel that my tragedy heightens their comedy and tragi-comedy, and grows itself more moving and intelligible from being mixed into the circumstance of the world by the circumstantial art of comedy.'[9] Yeats saw in Fenollosa's manuscript a similar function of the dramatic arts. the Noh plays were a series of stage images depicting, as Pound wrote, 'a complete service of life. We do not find, as we find in Hamlet, a certain situation or problem set out and analyzed. The Noh service presents, or symbolizes, a complete diagram of life and recurrence.'[10]

Yeats's first dance play, *At the Hawk's Well*, illustrates the extent to which Fenollosa's manuscript served as a catalyst in combining new scenic techniques, decorative arts, and formal acting. When Pound was editing the manuscript, Yeats saw the Abbey Company's London revival of two early plays — *The King's Threshold* (1914) and *On Baile's Strand* (1915). Ten years had passed since the first production of *The King's Threshold*, a play in which a series of debates is centred upon the main character. Charles Ricketts's new costumes seemed to Yeats to transform those lengthy harangues: 'The company never did the play so well, and such is the effect of costume that whole scenes got a new intensity, and passages or actions that seemed commonplace became powerful and moving.'[11] The backdrop, designed by his brother Jack B. Yeats (see Plate 12), placed the play within contemporary decorative design. No longer the depiction of a palace threshold, the new backcloth suggested a seashore by the high mountains of Gort, both the scene of the action and a controlling vision of the imagery in the dialogue. The revival of *On Baile's Strand*, staged with Rickett's 'Japanese' costumes (see Plate 13), delighted Yeats even more: 'The performance of *On Baile's Strand* has restored my confidence in myself.... The result is that I am full of new poems — dramatic and lyrical. All my mythological people have come alive again and I want to complete my heroic cycle.'[12] Encouraged by the revivals and his interest in Fenollosa's manuscript, Yeats returned to an early plan for a cycle of heroic plays. In the introduction to Pound's edition of *Certain Noble Plays of Japan*, he drew attention to the recent revivals: 'When I first began to write poetical plays for an Irish theatre I had to put away an ambition of helping to bring again to certain places their old sanctity or their romance. I could lay the scene of a play on Baile's Strand, but I found no pause in the hurried action for description of strand or sea or the great yew-tree that once stood there; and I could not in *The King's Threshold* find room, before I began the ancient story, to call up the shallow river and the few trees and rocky field of modern Gort.'[13]

At the Hawk's Well, begun soon after the revival of *On Baile's Strand*, illustrates how Yeats sharpened the focus of his theme through the stage image. Based on an early episode in the life of Cuchulain, the dance play is both a reworking of the *type* of conflict enacted in the final scenes of *On Baile's Strand* and a reenactment of the *moment* of distraction, when Cuchulain abandons the object of his greatest desire. In *On Baile's Strand* that moment of distraction is presented within the development of the narrative; Cuchulain, reminded amid cries of witchcraft of his oath to the King, rushes out to slay his own son. This dramatic situation, essentially a moment of inner conflict, is encumbered by the need to show cause and effect. In the dance play the situation is greatly simplified by linking the dialogue with the stage image. The image is taken from *On Baile's Strand*: Cuchulain is a 'fancy which runs as it were a swallow on the wind.' When pressed to swear allegiance to the King, Cuchulain picks up the same image:

> Nestlings of a high nest,
> Hawks that have followed me into the air
> And looked upon the sun, we'll out of this
> And sail upon the wind once more. (260)

The women's prayer combines this image of the hero, the irresponsible fancy on the wind, with the Shape Changers, the deadliest enemies of order

> Names whereby a man has known
> The threshold and the hearthstone,
> Gather on the wind and drive
> The women none can kiss and thrive,
> For they are but whirling wind,
> Out of memory and mind. (262)

These images, though, remain in the dialogue. Like the bird imagery in *Deirdre*, they do not shape the action of the play, which develops instead from the argument between Cuchulain and the King. In the dance play, however, the image becomes at the crucial moment of distraction a part of the stage image. Before the entrance of Cuchulain, the Musicians sing of the restless energy of the hero:

> 'Why should I sleep?' the heart cries,
> 'For the wind, the salt wind, the sea wind,
> Is beating a cloud through the skies;
> I would wander always like the wind.' (209)

Cuchulain arrives by a 'lucky wind under the sail.' These images of restless journey are brought directly into the stage action in the dance of distraction as the Guardian of the Well dances 'moving like a hawk' (see Plate 14):[14]

> Young Man. Run where you will,
>   Grey bird, you shall be perched upon my wrist.
>   Some were called queens and yet have been perched there.
>   [*The dance goes on.*
>
> First Musician [*speaking*]. I have heard the water plash; it comes, it comes.
>   Look where it glitters. He has heard the plash;
>   Look, he has turned his head.
>   [*The Guardian of the Well has gone out. The Young Man
>   drops his spear as if in a dream and goes out.* (217)

An Intimate Theatre

When Cuchulain returns to the empty well, he ignores the Old Man's plea. Like the changing breath of wind, he sets out on another journey, an unending battle with the Shape Changers, his defiant gesture serving as a type of heroic energy:

> Old Man. O, do not go! The mountain is accursed;
> Stay with me, I have nothing more to lose,
> I do not now deceive you.
>
> Young Man.   I will face them.
> *[He goes out, no longer as if in a dream, but shouldering his spear and calling:*
> He comes! Cuchulain, son of Sualtim, comes![15]   (218)

Cuchulain's parting gesture brings us to the other point of comparison between the dramatic forms of *On Baile's Strand* and *At the Hawk's Well*, the representation of a type of conflict. In the earlier play Yeats developed the conflict between Cuchulain and the King in the central episodes, mirrored in the Shakespearian double-plot of the Fool and the Blind Man.[16] the final scene, depicting the madness of Cuchulain, is enacted on stage in the Fool's mime, an invitation to the spectator's imagination and an acting out of 'the response Yeats hopes to elicit from his audience.'[17]

> Fool. O! he is fighting the waves!
> ....
> There, he has struck at a big one! He has struck the crown off it; he has made the foam fly. There again, another big one!
> ....
> There, he is down! He is up again. He is going out in the deep water. There is a big wave. It has gone over him. I cannot see him now. He has killed kings and giants, but the waves have mastered him, the waves have mastered him!
>   (277-278)

Cuchulain's heroism is further heightened and isolated by the tone of the final exit. The Fool and the Blind Man, whose actions throughout the play had served as an ironic counterpoint to the tragedy of the heroic characters, now rush out:

> Blind Man. There will be nobody in the houses. Come this way; come quickly! The ovens will be full. We will put our hands into the ovens.
> *[They go out.*   (278)

Cuchulain's fighting the waves, portrayed by his double the

Fool, is highly exciting in performance but emphasises only one aspect of the main conflict in the play. In *At the Hawk's Well* Yeats used a new combination of chorus and dramatic episode that allowed him to keep before the spectator an image of the central conflict while emphasizing here one aspect, there another. The oriental tradition described in the Fenollosa manuscript greatly interested Yeats: 'I go to Asia for a stage convention, for more formal faces, for a chorus that has no part in the action, and perhaps for those movements of the body copied from the marionette shows of the fourteenth century.'[18] Basing his Musicians on the Noh chorus 'which describes the scene and interprets their thought and never becomes as in the Greek theatre a part of the action,'[19] Yeats separated the function of the chorus and actor to a greater extent than he had done in *On Baile's Strand* or *Deirdre*. The opening song in *At the Hawk's Well* gives an image of the conflict and action which follows:

> I call to the eye of the mind
> A well long choked up and dry
> And boughs long stripped by the wind[20] (208)

Cuchulain and Conchubar in *On Baile's Strand* are replaced by universal types:[21] an Old Man, gnarled as the bare tree, and a Young Man, restless as the wind. The conflict will lead only to the loss of what they desire:

> First Musician [*singing*].
> The boughs of the hazel shake,
> The sun goes down in the west.
>
> Second Musician [*singing*].
> The heart would be always awake,
> The heart would turn to its rest. (209)

Throughout *At the Hawk's Well*, this central image of wind, tree, and well acts as a ballast to the narrative, reinforcing both the imagery in the dialogue and the stage action of the characters. After the final scene in which Cuchulain departs with the defiant gesture of the hero, spear in hand, leaving the Old Man crouched suppliant by the well, the Musicians' song frames these typical attitudes. As they unfold the cloth, they sing first of the Old Man, then of Cuchulain, then of their futility:

An Intimate Theatre

> Come to me, human faces,
> Familiar memories;
> I have found hateful eyes
> Among the desolate places,
> Unfaltering, unmoistened eyes.
>
> Folly alone I cherish,
> I choose it for my share;
> Being but a mouthful of air,
> I am content to perish;
> I am but a mouthful of sweet air.
>
> O lamentable shadows,
> Obscurity of strife!
> I choose a pleasant life
> Among indolent meadows;
> Wisdom must live a bitter life.   (219)

They sing at last as the empty well and leafless tree, drawing into the lyric the imagined stage setting. The lyric presents the completed action of the play, combining the Old Man and Young Man, the withered tree and fleeting wind. The hawk woman, their everlasting distraction, reappears on the opened cloth. (See Plates 14 and 15.) She is the reason behind the bitter, seemingly rhetorical question:

> Who but an idiot would praise
> Dry stones in a well?
> ....
> Who but an idiot would praise
> A withered tree?

Yeats's first dance play was thus a culmination of his work with Gordon Craig and the second Abbey Company, as well as a new departure in dramatic composition. The Fenollosa manuscript brought to life the tradition of presentational theatre, with its use of mask, costume, and dance, that Yeats acknowledged in his introduction to Pound's edition: 'We only believe in those thoughts which have been conceived not in the brain but in the whole body.'[22] The emphasis on presentation in the Noh began with Zeami, the first Noh master (1363-1443). Zeami described two kinds of Noh — Noh of the ear and eye and Noh of the mind — to indicate the two steps of seeing and understanding along the path towards the calm beauty of *yugen*. He taught his actors the underlying purpose of costume and movement: 'As conceived by Zeami, the mime might perhaps be compared to a continuous, ever-changing series of rhythmic colour patterns woven by the actor with the aid of gorgeous costumes and masks, the ultimate purpose of which is less to please the eye than to serve as a means of creating the *yugen* mood which is the very essence of the Noh drama.'[23] The effect of a Noh performance has been described by Oswald Sickert, writing to Yeats's friend Charles Ricketts during a visit to Japan in 1916:

> The best single moment I have seen was the dance of thanks to the fisherman who returns to the divine lady the Hagoromo, the robe without which even an angel cannot fly .... The thing may seem dull at first because at first it is the limitations the spectator feels; but the more these are exploited the less they are felt to be limitations, and the more they become a medium. The divine lady returned on her steps at great length and fully six times after I had thought I could not bear it another moment.... but I shall not recover from the longing she left when at last she floated backwards and under the fatal uplifted curtain.[24]

Masks and mime have become a convention of the modern theatre since Yeats's time, though they are not used in the manner of the Noh theatre. The mask, for instance, may be used to enhance the actor, whereas in the Noh the opposite is true. A Japanese actor undergoes a training to enhance the mask, as illustrated in the dressing ceremony that precedes a Noh performance. When the actor has put on the layers of kimono, he takes up his mask, holding it face to face as in a greeting. Attaching the mask in place, he stands before the great mirror off stage, studying his reflection, not to see himself in costume, but to see the character he will present to the audience. The Japanese say that each mask has its 'own individual kurai-dori, or position or level of quality,' which an actor presents to his audience, and they believe that 'not the person wearing the mask, but the mask itself sees.'[25] In Zeami's words, 'One's figure seen from the viewpoint of the audience is the "view from without", while one's own figure seen with one's own eyes is the "view from within."'[26] Fascinated by the special function of the Noh mask, Yeats suggested in *Four Plays for Dancers* that

> in the end one might write plays for certain masks. If some fine sculptor

should create for my 'Calvary', for instance, the masks of Judas, or Lazarus, and of Christ, would not this suggest other plays now, or many generations from now, and possess one cannot tell what philosophical virility. The mask, apart from its beauty, may suggest new situations at the moment when the old ones seem exhausted; 'The Only Jealousy of Emer' was written to find what dramatic effect one could get out of a mask, changed while the player remains upon the stage to suggest a change of personality.[27]

Though Yeats greatly admired the element of presentation in the Noh theatre, he adapted the Noh form to what is fundamentally a different type of drama. The combination of mask, costume, and stage movement could produce a more vivid and dynamic stage image than Yeats had devised for earlier plays, where the necessities of narrative overshadowed the expression of heroic action. The Noh form that most interested Yeats was the dream play, perfectly suited to isolate the moment and display the single heroic act. The dream play is essentially a drama of private revelation. The main character, the Shite, journeys to a place hallowed by past achievement or emotion. When questioned by the secondary character, the Waki, the Shite reveals the purpose of his journey and removes the costume that had disguised his identity. In the second part of the dream play the Waki observes, as in a dream or vision, the climactic dance of the Shite in which the past is reenacted. This dramatic revelation, the discovery through costume and mask of the lyric quality of heroic action displayed in the dance, led Yeats to adapt the form for three plays in *Four Plays for Dancers*. *The Only Jealousy of Emer* depicts the superhuman power of jealousy. *Calvary* presents the philosophical and religious oppositions at the centre of Yeats's concept of history. *The Dreaming of the Bones* follows most closely the form of the Noh dream play, while illustrating how Yeats adpated the form to depict a contemporary theme of political intransigence and unrelieved suffering.

The Only Jealousy of Emer is the most complicated of the early dance plays: the dying Cuchulain with his wife and mistress, the rivalry between the spirits Bricriu and Fand, and the struggle for possession of Cuchulain on the boundary between the living and the dead. To simplify the plot, Yeats adapted the second part of the Noh dream play to suggest an underlying resemblance — the possession by jealousy of each contender in the intrigue. In an early essay, 'The Moods,' Yeats described literature as wrought about a mood 'as the body is wrought about an invisible soul.' The artist should 'discover immortal moods in mortal desires, an undecaying hope in our trivial ambitions, a divine love in sexual passion.'[28] In 'Discoveries' he called the habitual moods 'careless and sudden.'[29] The changes of appearance made possible by masks enabled Yeats to depict sudden changes of mood while the masks themselves could suggest permanence of mood in contrast with the characters who wore them. In *Per Amica Silentia Lunae*, published after the completion of *The Only Jealousy of Emer*, Yeats described the quality of performance he saw in the mask: 'I thought the hero found hanging upon some oak of Dodona an ancient mask, where perhaps there lingered something of Egypt, and that he changed it to his fancy, touching it a little here and there, gilding the eyebrows or putting a gilt line where the cheek-bone comes; that when at last he looked out of its eyes he knew another's breath came and went within his breath upon the carven lips, and that his eyes were upon the instant fixed upon a visionary world: how else could the god have come to us in the forest?'[30]

The Only Jealousy of Emer is similar to the Noh play *Awoi no Uye*, included in the Fenollosa manuscript. (According to Japanese scholars, the subject of the play is the suffering of Lady Awoi, represented by a folded kimono at the front of the stage. A priest, attempting to exorcise her suffering, conjures up the Princess Rokujo in the mask of a female wraith, one of 'those whose spirits have temporarily left their bodies in a fury of jealousy or hatred.'[31] The Princess, a former mistress of Lady Awoi's prince, had been tormenting her rival in revenge. When a second priest arrives, Princess Rokujo reappears in the *hannya* mask of intense jealousy. Before the priests' prayers release her, she dances for fear and jealousy.) The version of *Awoi no Uye* that Pound edited, with admitted hesitation, was a different play. Working from a confused manuscript and with some direction from Yeats, he constructed a play based on the principle underlying *The Only Jealousy of Emer*. 'This play,' Pound announced, 'was written before Ibsen declared that life was a "contest with the phantoms of the mind."' Yeats read *Awoi no Uye* as a Japanese version of the Irish tales he and

An Intimate Theatre

Lady Gregory recorded in *Visions and Beliefs*, in which supernatural spirits seek power through possession of living bodies. Following Yeats's reading, Pound described *Awoi no Uye* as a representation of self-inflicted punishment:

> Awoi is tormented by her own passion, and this passion obsesses her first in the form of a personal apparition of Rokujo, then in demonic form....
>
> I do not know whether I can make the matter more plain or summarize it otherwise than by saying that the whole play is a dramatization, or externalization, of Awoi's jealousy. The passion makes her subject to the demon-possession. The demon first comes in a disguised and beautiful form. The prayer of the exorcist forces him first to appear in his true shape, and then to retreat.
>
> But the 'disguised and beautiful form' is not a mere abstract sheet of matter. It is a sort of personal or living mask, having a ghost life of its own; it is at once a shell of the princess, and a form, which is strengthened or made more palpable by the passion of Awoi.[32]

The notion that intense emotion could produce a 'living mask' or image of itself is the *modus operandi* of *The Only Jealousy of Emer*. Though the images from the spirit world, Fand and Bruicui, have knowledge denied the human characters, they lack the vitality to bring it to life. They draw upon the power and at the same time give shape to the vaguely understood feelings of the human characters. Yeats presents this struggle between power and knowledge in his adaptation of the Noh dream play.

In *The Only Jealousy of Emer* the controlling image of that struggle is the seashore, the border between the known and the unknown. As Yeats wrote in *Per Amica Silentia Lunae*, 'Our daily thought was certainly but the line of foam at the shallow edge of a vast luminous sea.'[33] This symbolic imagery recurs throughout the stage action and dialogue. As Cuchulain lies in stupor from fighting the waves, Emer tells his mistress Eithne Inguba:

> We're but two women struggling with the sea. (286)

The image of the seashore is used at first as part of the natural world, as in Eithne Inguba's attempt to rouse Cuchulain:

> I have never sent a message or called out,
> Scarce had a longing for your company

Players and Painted Stage

> But you have known and come ...
> ....
> Our passion had not chilled when we were parted
> On the pale shore under the breaking dawn. (286-287)

At this point there is a shift, as in the Noh play, from the natural to the supernatural, from the domestic scene to the spirit world. When Eithne Inguba embraces Cuchulain, she discovers the Bricrui, the Changeling spirit, come from the sea 'upon a bridleless horse.' (See Plate 16.) As she rushes out in horror, the hearth scene between wife and mistress is heightened to a vision of Emer's jealousy.

This vision is an adaptation of the second part of the Noh dream play in which the secondary character watches the culminating dance. In Yeats's play, the dance joins not the past and present of one character but the shared emotion of two — the dancer and Emer. This 'scheme of character relationships,' as Richard Taylor notes, is the basis of the play's 'Unity of Image.'[34] With special insight granted by Bricrui, Emer now watches Fand's dance of seduction round the figure of Cuchulain's ghost, now seen crouching by the shore. Like Eithne Inguba, Fand tries to draw him back with a kiss:

> Then kiss my mouth. Though memory
> Be beauty's bitterest enemy
> I have no dread, for at my kiss
> Memory on the moment vanishes:
> Nothing but beauty can remain. (292)

From Cuchulain's bed Bricrui cries out to Emer, describing the actions of the dance:

> Fool, fool!
> I am Fand's enemy come to thwart her will,
> And you stand gaping there. There is still time.
> Hear now the horses trample on the shore,
> Hear how they trample! She has mounted up.
> Cuchulain's not beside her in the chariot.
> There is still a moment left; cry out, cry out!
> Renounce him, and her power is at an end.
> Cuchulain's foot is on the chariot-step.
> Cry--
> Emer.   I renounce Cuchulain's love for ever. (294)

An Intimate Theatre

Emer's cry is a dramatisation of the 'bargain' Yeats described in *Per Amica Silentia Lunae*: 'We can satisfy in life a few of our passions and each passion a little, and our characters indeed but differ because no two men bargain alike. The bargain, the compromise, is always threatened, and when it is broken we become mad or hysterical or in some way deluded; and so when a starved or banished passion shows in a dream we, before awaking, break the logic that had given it the capacity of action and throw it into chaos again.'[35] Emer's renunciation breaks the vision. The masks are changed again and Cuchulain wakes, reaching for Eithne Inguba. This sudden shift joins the mood in the dream with the mood at the hearth. Emer's jealousy, the changeling's jealousy, Fand's jealousy, are all given shape, then all banished. The Musicians' closing song, Emer's address to Fand, suggests the failure even of Eithne Inguba:

> What makes your heart so beat?
> What man is at your side?
> When beauty is complete
> Your own thought will have died
> And danger not be diminished;
> Dimmed at three-quarter light,
> When moon's round is finished
> The stars are out of sight.
>
> O bitter reward
> Of many a tragic tomb!
> And we though astonished are dumb
> Or give but a sigh and a word,
> A passing word.[36]   (296)

The Only Jealousy of Emer illustrates the possibility the Noh dream play offered for the representation of the inner world, the imaginative life in the midst of daily circumstance, and of the antimony between the living and the dead. Yeats considered the dream play, sculpted as it were from mask, costume, and dance, a major form of the expressive style in art. Objecting to the restless 'curiosity' portrayed in the realistic style, he drew attention to the opposite effect in his essay on the Noh: 'In poetical painting and in sculpture the face seems the nobler for lacking curiosity, alert attention, all that we sum up under the famous word of the realists, 'vitality'. It is even possible that being is only possessed completely by the dead, and that it is some knowledge of this that makes us gaze with so much emotion upon the face of the Sphinx or of Buddha.'³⁷

The connections Yeats drew between sculpture, mask, and the world of the dead were in part a restatement of Gordon Craig's controversial essay 'The Actor and the Über-Marionette' (1907), in which Craig urged the European theatre to return to the use of mask and dance. The modern marionette, he insisted, had descended from 'stone images of the old temples — he is today a rather degenerate form of a god.'³⁸ Craig called for new training for actors, similar to the tradition of the Noh theatre. Contemporary European acting was based on 'accident,' not training, the actor controlled by his emotions, not his mind: 'The whole nature of man tends towards freedom; he therefore carries the proof in his own person that as *material* for the Theatre he is useless.... In the beginning the human body was not used as material in the Art of the Theatre. In the beginning the emotions of men and women were not considered as a fit exhibition for the multitude.'³⁹ Craig wanted a 'new form of acting, consisting for the main part of symbolid gesture.' His description of the new style of theatre, though more obscure than Yeats's pronouncement that 'being is only possessed by the dead,' is written in the same terms — spirits, shades, nonhuman vitality, Death: 'Shades — spirits seem to me to be more beautiful, and filled with more vitality than men or women.... For, looking too long upon life, may one not find all this to be not the beautiful, nor the mysterious, nor the tragic, but the dull, the melodramatic, and the silly.... But from that mysterious, joyous, and superbly complete life which is called Death — that life of shadow and of unknown shapes, where all cannot be blackness and fog as it is supposed, but vivid colour, vivid light, sharp-cut form.... From this idea of death... can come so vast an inspiration, that with unhesitating exultation I leap forward to it.'⁴⁰ Considered in the context of the debate surrounding contemporary naturalistic drama, Yeats's and Craig's views lose some of their apparent strangeness and morbidity. The emphasis on 'death' rather than 'life' is an emphasis on the convention of masks, costumes, and symbolic characters rather than the naturalistic mode of acting and stage setting. In

Yeats's words, 'Our unimaginative arts are content to set a piece of the world as we know it in a place by itself, to put their photographs as it were in a plush or plain frame, but the arts which interest me, while seeming to separate from the world and us a group of figures, images, symbols, enable us to pass for a few moments into a deep of the mind that has hitherto been too subtle for our habitation.'[41]

In *At the Hawk's Well* and *The Only Jealousy of Emer*, Yeats developed the central image in the dialogue into a stage image incorporating both language and movement, using the stage image as a focus for the emotional quality of the action. In the structure of the Noh ghost play, Yeats acknowledged a type of adventure similar to the Irish tradition: 'The adventure itself is often the meeting with ghost, god or goddess at some holy place or much-legended tomb; and god, goddess or ghost reminds me at times of our own Irish legends and beliefs, which once, it may be, differed little from those of the Shinto worshipper.'[42] The Noh play, as Yeats understood it, was a meeting place between the natural and supernatural, but he did not follow the Noh form in its depiction of the revelation of the supernatural and the resulting *yugen*, or calm beauty. As the last two dance plays vividly illustrate, Yeats chose rather to depict the unrelieved conflict between the two.

Calvary is a powerful play of unresolved conflict, a portrayal of the opposition Yeats believed to be at the root of history. Christ, representing the birth of a civilisation come to defeat the classical world, dreams back those he thought he had saved. As Yeats explained, 'The conception of the play is derived from the world-wide belief that the dead dream back, for a certain time, through the more personal thoughts and deeds of life': 'I have surrounded him with the images of those He cannot save, not only with the birds, who have served neither God nor Caesar, and await for none or a different saviour, but with Lazarus and Judas and the Roman soldiers for whom He has died in vain.... I have therefore represented in Lazarus and Judas types of that intellectual despair that lay beyond His sympathy...'[43] The structure of *Calvary*, three episodes between Christ and the others, with lyric interludes, acts as a prism to throw the philosophical conflict into three visual patterns embodied in the actors' stage movements. This repetition is similar to the rhythm Yeats admired in the Noh drama: 'I have lately studied certain of these dances, with Japanese players, and I notice that their ideal of beauty, unlike that of Greece and like that of pictures from Japan and China, makes them pause at moments of muscular tension. The interest is not in the human form but in the rhythm to which it moves, and the triumph of their art is to express the rhythm in its intensity.'[44]

Yeats represented the conflict between Christ and the others as horizontal and vertical movement: Christ, upright and motionless, surrounded by the others. This visual representation can be immediate and effective in performance, especially when the audience's knowledge of Christian tradition adds force to the impact of Yeats's interpretation. The controlling image of *Calvary* is given in the opening lyric:

> Although fish leap, the white heron
> Shivers in a dumbfounded dream.   (449)

The movement suggested in the lyric — the motionless heron surrounded by everchanging nature — is enacted by the Musicians, as the First Musician holds up the hawk design at the centre of the cloth (Plate 15), while the other two unfold, then fold the black cloth, 'pacing with a rhythmic movement of the arms towards the First Musician.'[45] Their folding of the cloth is like the image of change in the final stanza of the song; like the hawk on the cloth, the heron remains motionless, caught up in his reflected image, though the moon disappear, the reflection vanish.

> First Musician.
>   But that the full is shortly gone
>   And after that is crescent moon,
>   It's certain that the moon-crazed heron
>   Would be but fishes' diet soon.
>
> Second Musician.
>   God has not died for the white heron.   (450)

In the three dream episodes of *Calvary*, Christ sees himself diminish like the reflected image, seeing at last his powerlessness 'to save those who can live without salvation.'[46] This conflict between two kinds of personality, producing in Yeats's view the great ebb and flow of civilisations, is built into the

Robert Gregory's design for the 1906 Abbey Theatre production of W. B. Yeats' Deirdre showing the use of tied curtains rather than naturalistic stage sets to suggest the interior of a room with a view beyond.

Bedford Lemere's 1891 photograph of the old Empire Music Hall, Newcastle, which has been used by Richard Southern as an example of the 'typical' Victorian theatre. Its naturalistic backdrop of a street scene stems, however, from the tradition of tragic, comic and satyric stage settings of the ancient Roman theatre described by Viturvius and interpreted by Serlio (Plate 3a).

Serlio's wood engraving of Scene Tragica *(published 1566)*, admired by Gordon Craig as a model of the previous age of stage design. Inspired by Serlio's wood engravings of the ancient Roman theatre, Craig considered his own work as the new age of stage design.

Gordon Craig's first drawing for Scene, 1906, copied from the original and prepared for a wood engraving by the author, 1924.

A moment of arrested motion in Gordon Craig's conception of Scene.

Gordon Craig and his model stage, England 1910. W. B. Yeats ordered a model stage for the Abbey Theatre after being given a demonstration by Craig.

Robert Gregory's drawing for the set of the 1906 Abbey Theatre production of The Hour-Glass *showing the furniture that Yeats considered a distraction.*

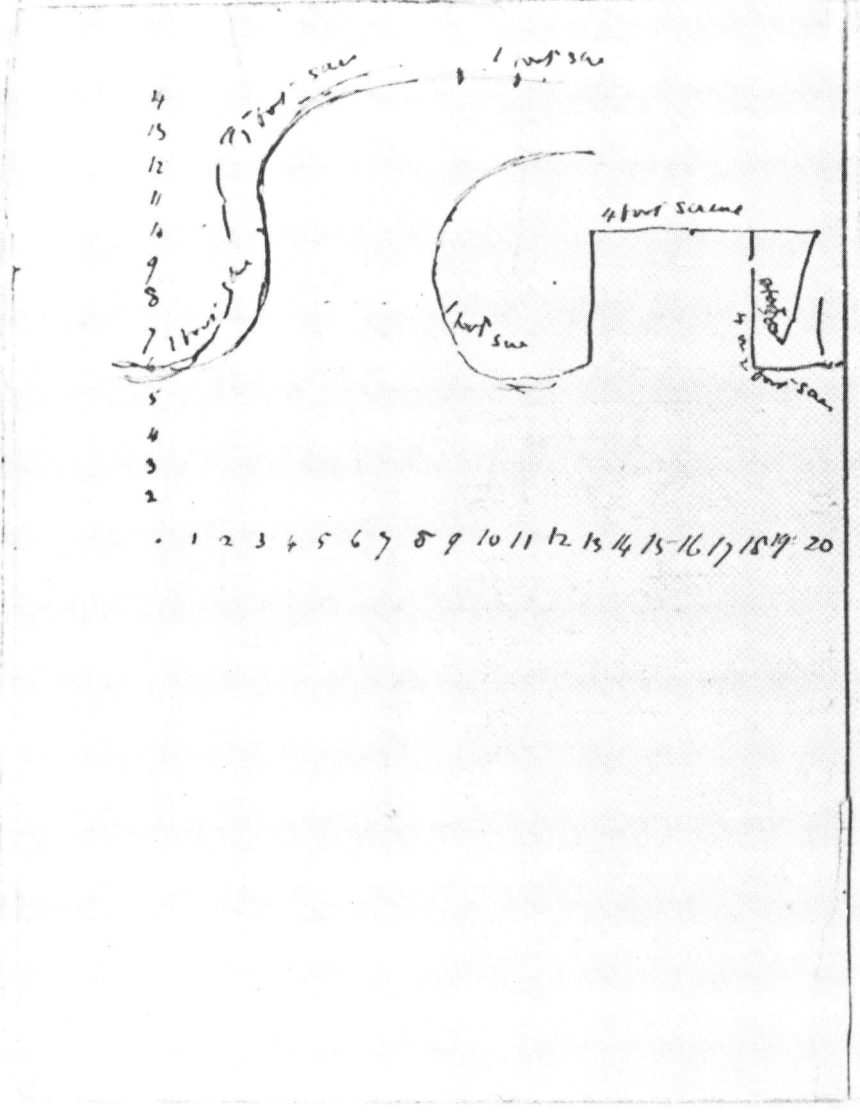

A page from W. B. Yeats's Notebook of Scene Arrangements, 1910, showing his sketch for the arrangement of Gordon Craig's screens on the stage of the Abbey Theatre for the 1912 production of The Hour-Glass. *(See Plate 9).*

Gordon Craig's wood engraving of the Mask of the Blind Man, W. B. Yeats's On Baile's Strand, *1911*.

Gordon Craig's sketch, 1910, of W. B. Yeats's arrangement of screens for the production of The Hour-Glass at the Abbey Theatre, 1911. (See Plate 7).

Gordon Craig's wood-engraving of the Mask of the Fool, W. B. Yeats's The Hour-Glass, *1911.*

Gordon Craig's costume design for The Fool, *W. B. Yeats's* The Hour-Glass, *1911, with the domino mask (See Plate 10), shears and money bag sleeve.*

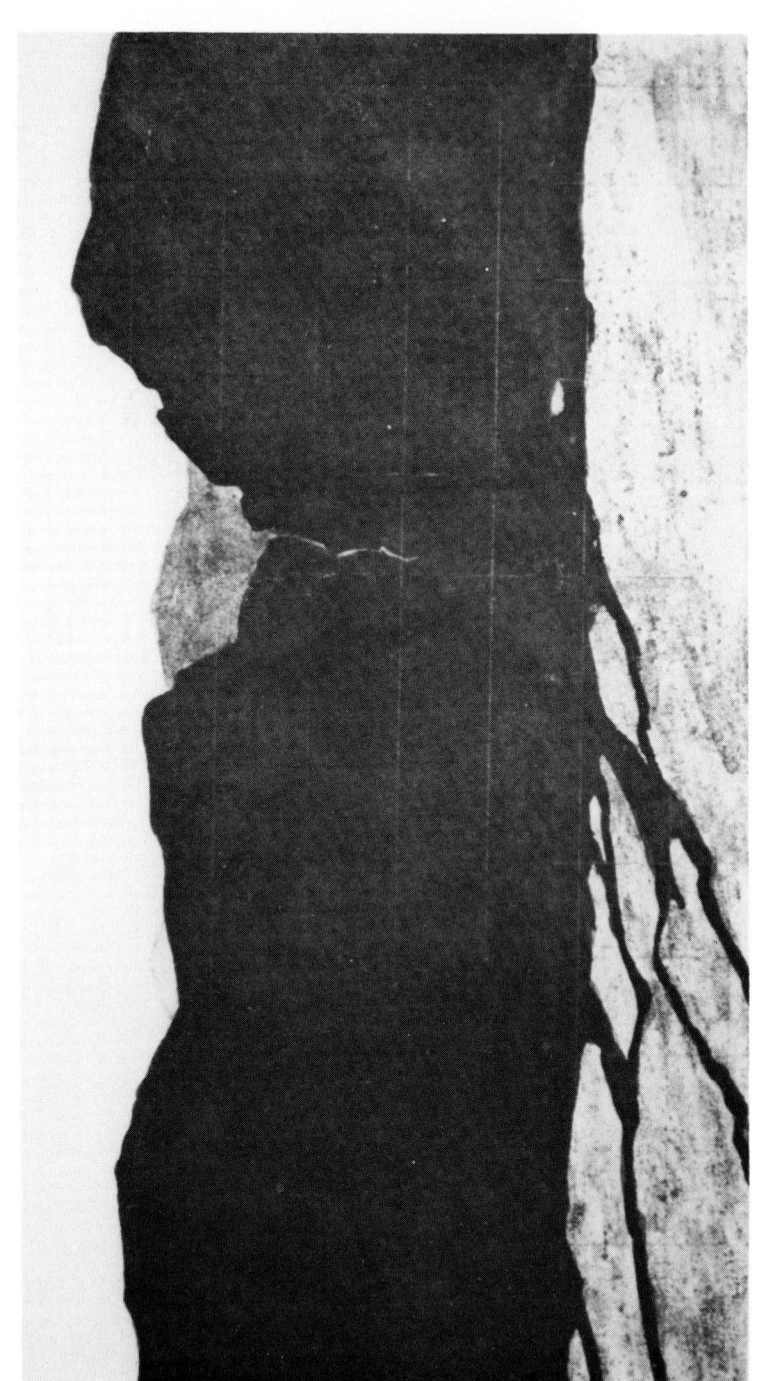

Jack B. Yeats's design for a backcloth, 1913, for W. B. Yeats's The King's Threshold, 1914, on which the seashore and mountains near Gort are depicted in a new decorative style much admired by W. B. Yeats.

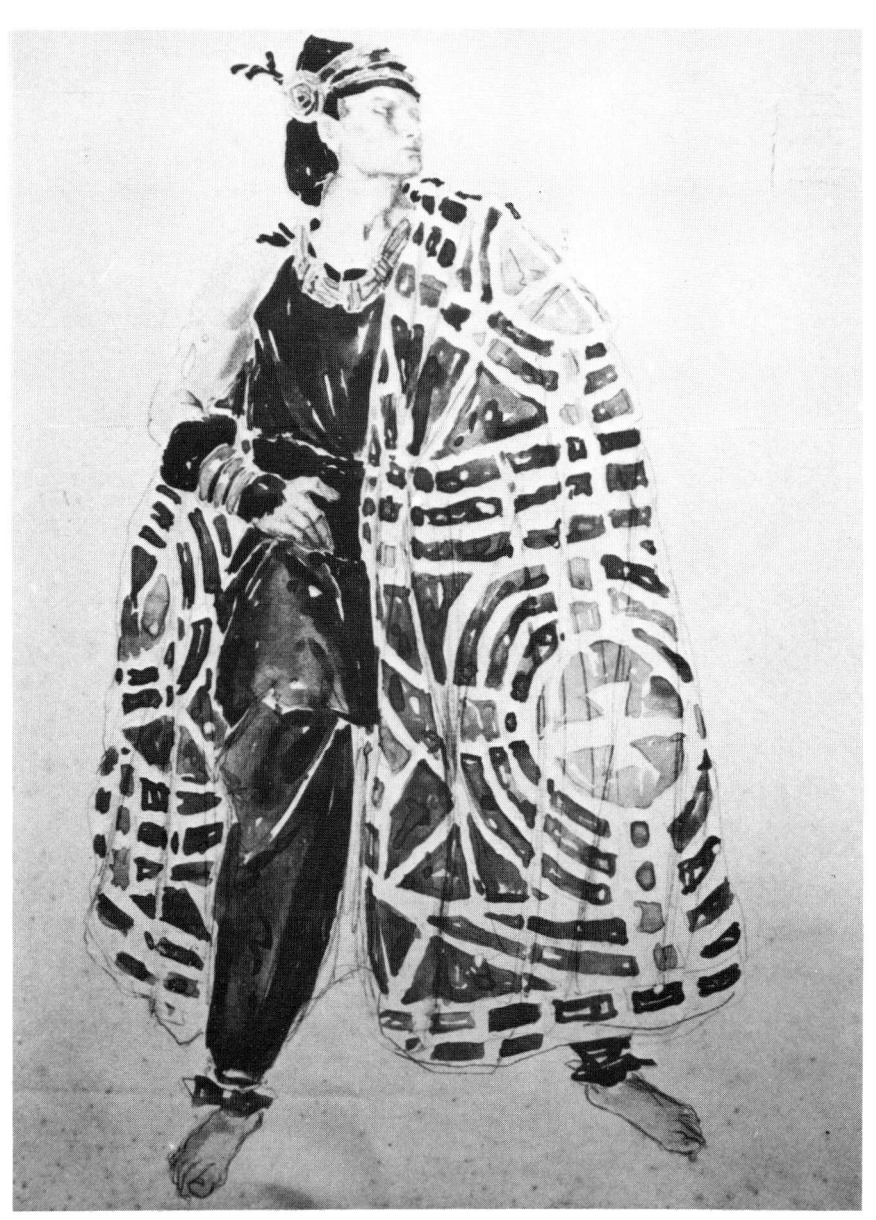

Charles Ricketts' costume design for Cuchulain in W. B. Yeats's On Baile's Strand, *1915.*

The Japanese dancer, Michio Itoh, as Guardian of the Well in W. B. Yeats's At the Hawk's Well, *London 1916, photograph by Alvin Langdon Coburn.*

Edmund Dulac's design for the Musicians' Cloth in At the Hawk's Well, 1916.

The discovery of the Changeling in W. B. Yeats's The Only Jealousy of Emer, *in Albert van Dalsum's production, Amsterdam, 1926. Hildo Krop's masks for the 1922 and 1926 Amsterdam productions inspired W. B. Yeats to rewrite the play as a dance drama,* Fighting the Waves.

An Intimate Theatre

stage movement of *Calvary*, a pattern of 'contrasts between the active and fixed, personal and impersonal, suffering which reaches out in gloating and accusation and suffering which is withdrawn and symbolic.'[47] In the first scene, the dialogue shapes the stage movement. Lazarus complains of being dragged from his tomb

> ... as boys drag out
> A rabbit when they have dug its hole away .   (452)

He sees that Christ

> ... will blind with light the solitude
> That death has made; you will disturb that corner
> Where I had thought I might lie safe for ever.   (452)

As Christ stands erect, holding his cross, his words reinforce the vertical movement:

> But I have conquered death,
> And all the dead shall be raised up again.   (452)

While Christ stands motionless as the heron, Lazarus departs, ironically to seek out

> ... the desert places where there is nothing
> But howling wind and solitary birds.   (452)

In a brief musical interlude the Musicians foreshadow the final crucifixion, joining that image with the earlier one of the heron. Their song describes Christ's gesture — half-consolation, half-crucifixion — as he dreams the women:

> He holds His right arm out, and on His arm
> Their lips are pressed and their tears fall; and now
> They cast them on the ground before His dirty
> Blood-dabbled feet and clean them with their hair.
>
> [*Sings*]
> Take but His love away
> Their love becomes a feather
> Of eagle, swan or gull,
> Or a drowned heron's feather
> Tossed hither and thither
> Upon the bitter spray
> .And the moon at the full.   (453)

Christ's second meeting with Judas requires a mode of acting

Players and Painted Stage

embodying what Yeats called 'curiosity' and nervous attention to naturalistic detail. As Judas argues for personal power, the rhythm of the verse suggests the movement:

> It was decreed that somebody betray you —
> I'd thought of that — but not that I should do it,
> I the man Judas, born on such a day,
> In such a village, such and such his parents;
> Nor that I'd go with my old coat upon me
> To the High Priest, and chuckle to myself
> As people chuckle when alone, and do it
> For thirty pieces and no more, no less,
> And neither with a nod nor a sent message,
> But with a kiss upon your cheek. I did it,
> I, Judas, and no other man, and now
> You cannot even save me.   (454-455)

Like the image of heron and fish, Christ and Judas stand side by side — the one still and impersonal, the other curious and inquiring:

> Judas.   ... And now
> Is there a secret left I do not know,
> Knowing that if a man betrays a God
> He is the stronger of the two?
>
> Christ.   But if
> 'Twere the commandment of that God himself,
> That God were still the stronger.   (454)

The stage image again reinforces the conflict. Though Christ dismisses the man who had tried to free himself, they are joined together.

> Christ. Begone from me.
> [*Three Roman Soldiers have entered.*
>
> First Roman Soldier. He has chosen to hold up the cross.
> [*During what follows, Judas holds up the
> cross while Christ stands with His arms
> stretched out upon it.*   (455)

Christ's meeting with the Roman soldiers is the first portrayal of conflict in *Calvary*. Lazarus and Judas denied Christ's love, the soldiers remark:

> To know that he has nothing that we need
> Must be a comfort to him.   (456)

52

An Intimate Theatre

They entertain Christ with the dance of the dice-throwers,[48] dancing round the cross, as in the Musicians' lyric fish leap about the crazed heron. Their dancing is a recapitulation of the argument of the previous episodes and, as Katharine Worth notes, 'a spectacular dancing out of the image of change and chance with which the play began'[49]

> Second Roman Soldier.   In the dance
>   We quarrel for a while, but settle it
>   By throwing dice, and after that, being friends,
>   Join hand to hand and wheel about the cross.
> *[They dance.*
> Christ. My Father, why hast Thou forsaken Me?   (456)

The pattern of this dance is gathered into the images in the final song. The single hawk figure reappears on the black cloth, like the recurring image of the heron. The image acts as a constellation of meaning — a single shape suggesting both Christ's isolation and the opposite self-absorption of the others. Yeats used the 'bird-symbolism in these songs to increase the objective loneliness of Christ by contrasting it with a loneliness, opposite in kind, that unlike His can be, whether joyous or sorrowful, sufficient to itself.'[50] In the closing song the Musicians sing of birds in flight — of the lonely seabird, like Lazarus heading for his tomb, 'Under a great wave's hollowing crest'; the ger-eagle, like Judas, 'content with his savage heart'; last year's cygnets who, like the dancing soldiers, fling 'White wing out beside white wing.' Christ's dream ends, the loneliness and sense of failure remaining to the last. As the song ends, the hawk design, too, disappears, as the cloth is folded into itself:

> First Musician.
>   But where have last year's cygnets gone?
>   The lake is empty; why do they fling
>   White wing out beside white wing?
>   What can a swan need but a swan?
> Second Musician.
>   God has not appeared to the birds.   (457)

In *The Dreaming of the Bones*, the last of the early dance plays, Yeats adapted the Noh dream play for the expression of

Players and Painted Stage

emotion radically different from the calm beauty of *yugen*. Written after the Easter Uprising, *The Dreaming of the Bones* — like Yeats's *Cathleen ni Houlihan*, Synge's *Playboy of the Western World*, Lady Gregory's *Rising of the Moon*, and O'Casey's *Juno and the Paycock* — is a portrayal of the emotional quality underlying an episode in Irish politics. Yeats based the play on Pound's version of *Nishikigi*, in which a travelling priest meets the ghosts of lovers; the woman had refused an offer of marriage, but their former separation and suffering is resolved as they create in a dance their wedding night. What Yeats admired in *Nishikigi* was a "playing upon a single metaphor, as deliberate as the echoing rhythm of line in Chinese and Japanese painting."[51] In *The Dreaming of the Bones* the central image is one of circling, filling up — cloud in the valley, wine in the cup — that creates the feeling of anticipation; the image is, as David Clark has pointed out, 'analogous to the direction the action takes':[52]

> First Musician [*or all three Musicians, singing*].
>   Why does my heart beat so?
>   Did not a shadow pass?
>   It passed but a moment ago.
>   Who can have trod in the grass?
>   What rogue is night-wandering?
>   Have not old writers said
>   That dizzy dreams can spring
>   From the dry bones of the dead?
>   And many a night it seems
>   That all the valley fills
>   With those fantastic dreams.
>   They overflow the hills,
>   So passionate is a shade,
>   Like wine that fills to the top
>   A grey-green cup of jade,
>   Or maybe an agate cup.   (433-434)

In contrast with *Nishikigi*, Yeats's play expresses the violent mood of the 1916 Easter Uprising. The image of circling controls the mounting emotion as the Irish Republican Army soldier and the ghosts of Diarmuid and Dervorgilla circle round in the midst of the audience. When the ghosts reveal their identity, the soldier's horror is given further expression in the final dance:

An Intimate Theatre

> They have drifted in the dance from rock to rock.
> They have raised their hands as though to snatch the sleep
> That lingers always in the abyss of the sky
> Though they can never reach it. A cloud floats up
> And covers all the mountain-head in a moment;
> But now it lifts and they are swept away.
>   [*The Stranger and the Young Girl go out.*
> I had always yielded and forgiven it all —
> Terrible the temptation and the place! (444)

In this denial of forgiveness lies the difference between the Japanese ghost play and Yeats's dance play.[53] *Nishikigi* ends not in denial but in fulfilment, as the priest calls for the dance:

> Shite
> Happy at last and well-starred,
> Now comes the eve of betrothal:
> We meet for the wine-cup.
>
> Chorus
> How glorious the sleeves of the dance,
> That are like snow-whirls!
>
> Shite
> Tread out the dance.[54]

None of Yeats's plays expresses this fulfilled emotion. In the Noh play the priest is a witness, not a protagonist; in Yeats's plays even the dance is part of the conflict: the hawk dances to lure Cuchulain from the miraculous well, Fand dances to entice him from Emer, the Roman soldiers dance round Christ.[55] This is the crucial difference between the view of life represented in the Noh theatre and in Yeats's dance plays — in the one, the creation of *yugen* through brilliant revelation of emotion, in the other, the creation of a quality of energy and lyrical feeling discovered in conflict.

    The transformation of Yeats's theatre that can be seen in the first dance plays is a testament to the effect of the Fenollosa manuscript. T. S. Eliot, after seeing the 1916 production of *At the Hawk's Well* in Lady Cunard's drawing room, acknowledged the importance of Yeats's new dramatic form in his fragment 'Sweeney Agonistes.'[56] The dance plays freed Yeats from the dominant naturalistic mode of the Abbey, though it would be wrong to assume that they mark a final break with the Abbey Company and its audience during the upheaval of the First World War and the Irish Troubles. Far from abandoning the Abbey, Yeats continued his work as a fund raiser and adviser for new scripts. His versions of Sophocles' Oedipus plays in the late 1920s, his naturalistic drama *Words Upon the Window-Pane* (1930), and a further series of dance plays based on his work with Ninette de Valois were all popular successes at the Abbey.[57] Written both for the main stage and for the smaller stage of the Peacock Theatre, these plays show Yeats's continuing experiment, building upon the dance plays, with new dramatic forms. *The Player Queen*, written for the main Abbey stage and for a large cast, can be used to show that Yeats's dance plays mark not a final break but the consolidation of a dramatic form for the proscenium theatre.

The Player Queen was written and revised during the period 1907-1922, the years of the first dance plays.[58] Two aspects of the final version indicate Yeats's interests at the time of the first draft: the use of the stage setting to reinforce the dialogue, and the dramatisation (as in *Deirdre*) of his theory of the Mask. As in *The Hour-Glass*, varying degrees of stage lighting accompany the development of the theme. Yeats wrote the original version using the model stage with folding screens that Craig had given Yeats for the Abbey (Plate 5).[59] Two of Craig's contemporary woodcuts suggest the range of expression in *The Player Queen*, from darkened menacing forms of 'In Italy' (Plate 17) to the vividly lit scene in 'Troy Burning' (Plate 21). The opening dialogue makes explicit the expressive quality of the setting. Two masked actors lean out from windows.

> First Old Man. Can you see the Queen's castle? You have better sight than I.
>
> Second Old Man. I can just see it rising over the tops of the houses yonder on its great rocky hill.
>
> First Old Man. Is the dawn breaking? Is it touching the tower?
>
> Second Old Man. It is beginning to break upon the tower, but these narrow streets will be dark for a long while. [*A pause.*] Do you hear anything? You have better hearing than I.
>
> First Old Man. No, all is quiet.

An Intimate Theatre

> Second Old Man. At least fifty passed by an hour since, a crowd of fifty men walking rapidly.
>
> (387-388)

The second act of *The Player Queen*, set in the Throne Room of the castle, also begins in deep shadow. By the end of the play, as the actors choose new roles, the stage is fully lit: what had begun in shadow and rehearsal concludes in power and performance. As in Yeats's phases of the moon, the light illuminates the images of completed beauty.[60]

Despite Yeats's claim that it was 'the only play of mine which has not its scene laid in Ireland,'[61] *The Player Queen* is an adaptation of themes from his early Abbey work. The controversy over the Irish national image reappears in Septimus' argument with the 'bad, popular poets,' while a rumour linking the Queen with a Unicorn provides the play with its own context of political interpretation.[62] The Prime Minister's attempt to save the Queen and calm the citizens through a performance of travelling players is a high-spirited parody of Yeats's early years at the Abbey Theatre:

> Prime Minister:
>
> The leading lady is lost, you say, and there is some unintelligible reason why nobody can take her place; but I know what you are all driving at — you object to the play I have chosen. You want some dull, poetical thing, full of long speeches. I will have that play and no other. The rehearsal must begin at once....
>
> (403-404)

Much of the first act bears the mark of work repeatedly revised but not yet coherent. Not until the final scene does Yeats succeed as in the dance plays in joining language and movement in a crystallisation of the character of Septimus. During his quarrel with the 'popular poets' and the defence of the Unicorn, Septimus has acted as a self-proclaimed prophet. As in Gordon Craig's woodcut, 'Hamlet: An Actor' (Plate 18), he is inspired by the role: 'My breast-feathers thrust out and my white wings buoyed up with divinity.'[63] Biblical allusion reinforces the part:

> Carry me, support me, drag me, roll me, pull me, or sidle me along, but bring me where I may sleep in comfort. Bring me to a stable — my Saviour was content with a stable.

....

> Robbed, so to speak; naked, so to speak — bleeding, so to speak — and they pass by on the other side of the street.
>
> (391)

Septimus' new role is completed by the arrival of the Old Beggar, who brays at the change of crown because 'it is the donkey that carried Christ into Jerusalem, and that is why it knows its rightful sovereign.' At the close of the first act, Septimus' role is developed into a full stage image. He and the Old Beggar set off for the castle; the dialogue controls the actors' mime as the self-proclaimed saviour of the Unicorn leans for support upon the beggar-donkey:

> The Old Beggar. I want straw to lie down on.
>
> Septimus. It is no doubt better that I should bleed to death. For that way, my friend, I shall disgrace Happy Tom and Peter of the Purple Pelican, but it is necessary that I shall die somewhere where my last words can be taken down. I am therefore in need of your support.
> ....
> Septimus. Ah! you are inspired. Then we are indeed brothers. Come, I will rest upon your shoulder and we will mount the hill side by side.
>
> (401)

The theme of *The Player Queen* is fully worked out in the second act, where a jealous intrigue between Decima, Nona, and Septimus is built upon the scaffolding of Yeats's theory of the Mask. As Decima says of Nona, 'I threw away a part and I threw away a man — and she has picked up both.' Yeats has described his first attempt in 1907 'to write a poetical play where every character became an example of the finding or not finding of what I have called the Antithetical Self.'[64] Among Yeats's examples of his theory was Mrs. Patrick Campbell's portrayal of Deirdre, which inspired the first version of *The Player Queen*.[65] The major revisions were made during the following decade, and the flaws appear to stem from the predominance of the theory over the dramatic situation. As Rupin Desai says, 'Too much of the author is present everywhere for it to achieve a life of its own.'[66] Desai's illuminating discussion of the analogies between *The Player Queen* and *Hamlet* points to another example of Yeats's theory of the Mask. Desai notes the deep impression made upon Yeats by Henry Irving's performance as Hamlet, which Yeats later

An Intimate Theatre

described as 'an image of heroic self-possession for the poses of youth and childhood to copy, a combatant of the battle within myself.'[67] Desai's discussion could be further supported by the great interest Yeats showed in Gordon Craig's work for Stanislavski's 1911 production of *Hamlet* for the Moscow Art Theatre (Plate 20). Hamlet's continual meditation upon his role in the unfolding drama is suggested by Craig's woodcut, 'Hamlet and Daemon' (Plate 19), one of the woodcuts in an exhibition of Craig's stage designs that Yeats helped arrange in Dublin in 1913. As in Hamlet's decision to join Laertes in the sword play or Deirdre's premeditated choice, the women in *The Player Queen* move decisively towards a new role: the Queen, a saint; Nona, Decima's part as Noah's wife; and Decima, nothing less than Queen.

Yeats used the elements of mask, costume, and dance to full effect in the final scene of *The Player Queen*. Drawing upon his work with Gordon Craig and the dance plays, he was able to express the sudden shift of personality through these elements. As Katharine Worth points out, 'By the end of the play, the theatrical mode has become universal; there are no non-actors, only different degrees of skill and self-consciousness in performance.'[68] Yeats's theme appears in an entry in the 1909 Diary: 'Is it simply the doctrine of the Mask? The choosing of some one Mask? Hardly for that would be the imitation of Christ in a new form. Is it becoming Mask after Mask.... the nature of the men seems to prepare for a continual change — a phantasmagoria, one day one god and the next another.'[69] Both the Old Beggar's braying and the players' repertoire — 'The Fall of Troy' and 'The Tragical History of Noah's Deluge' — suggest a turn of events. Decima, dressed at last as the Queen, picks upon the mask of Noah's sister, discarded when Septimus carried away the masks and costumes of the travelling players. It is the mask of a woman destroyed, and as she addresses the dancers, on the fully lit stage, the Player Queen completes the image:

> You are banished and must not return upon pain of death, and yet not one of you shall be poorer because banished. That I promise. But you have lost one thing that I will not restore. A woman player has left you. Do not mourn her. She was a bad, headstrong, cruel woman, and seeks destruction somewhere and with some man she knows

nothing of; such a woman they tell me that this mask would well become, this foolish, smiling face! Come, dance.
[*They dance, and at certain moments she cries* 'Good-bye, good-bye' *or else* 'Farewell'. *And she throws them money.*][70]
(430)

By the time Yeats developed the form of the dance play, he saw clearly how his own work stood in relation to the predominant naturalism of the Abbey Theatre. In an open letter to Lady Gregory, 'A People's Theatre' (1919), he explained the difference in style as a difference in perception: 'We stand on the margin between wilderness and wilderness, that which we observe through our senses and that which we can experience only, and our art is always the description of one or the other.'[71] The development of the full stage image, begun during work with Gordon Craig and strengthened by adaptations of elements in the Noh drama, was done always with a view in mind of the audience, whether the Abbey audience or a smaller drawing room gathering. This link between audience and performance was based on Yeats's understanding of the nature of the image, its source and its effect on the spectator. Seen in this light, the stage image developed in the dance plays is not an exotic borrowed form but rather a central part of the controversy surrounding modern poetry.

That controversy was brought to focus in Pound's definition of the poetic image as a presentation of 'an intellectual and emotional complex in an instant of time.'[72] During his work with the Fenollosa manuscript Pound was struck by Yeats's interest in images that led beyond the immediate moment, 'images more powerful than sense.'[73] In the introduction to *Awoi No Uye*, Pound explained that certain events would combine to help 'the spirit world to manifest itself concretely. Western students of ghostly folk-lore would tell you that the world of spirits is fluid about seeking shape. I do not wish to dogmatize on these points.'[74] A hint of the disagreement over poetic image appeared in Pound's 'Prolegomena' for the second issue of *Poetry Review* (February 1912): 'I believe that the proper and perfect symbol is the natural object, that if a man uses 'symbols' he must so use them that their symbolic function does not obtrude; so that *a* sense, and the poetic quality of the passage, is not lost to those who do not understand the symbol as such, to whom, for instance, a hawk is a hawk.'[75] Yeats preferred the image rooted in tradition, the image combining the single moment of Pound's 'intellectual and emotional complex' with a shared traditional meaning. Their disagreement is clearly illustrated in their views of the American painter James McNeill Whistler.

When Whistler's work was exhibited at the Tate Gallery in September 1912, Pound saw in his style a visual analogue to his own poetry: 'From Whistler and the Japanese, or Chinese, the "world", that is to say, the fragment of the English-speaking world which spreads itself into print, learned to enjoy "arrangements" of colours and masses.'[76] Pound assumed that his readers took 'pleasure in "Whistler and the Japanese,"' but that assumption was no longer shared by Yeats. In 'Art and Ideas' (1913) Yeats recalled that his early circle of writers 'all silently obeyed a canon that had become powerful for all the arts since Whistler, in the confidence of his American *naivete*, had told everybody that Japanese painting had no literary ideas.'[77] Though Yeats had once 'found encouragement by noticing all round me painters who were ridding their pictures, and indeed their minds, of literature,'[78] he now thought better of it. Dismissing his early verse as sentimental and formless, he found its effect unsatisfactory: 'Yet those delighted senses, when I had got from them all I could, left me discontented. Impressions that needed so elaborate a record did not seem like the handiwork of those careless old writers one imagines squabbling over a mistress, or riding on a journey, or drinking round a tavern fire, brisk and active men.'[79] This image of brisk and active men stands in opposition to Pound's arrangements of colours and masses. Pound's poetic image is meant to embody a unique experience, Yeats's image a shared experience, an emotion 'self-conscious and reminiscent, always associating itself with pictures and poems.'[80] Setting himself against Imagism and the modern movement, Yeats described Pound's image with Blake's phrase, 'the fall of man into his own circumference.' The intention of the Abbey founders, and Yeats's belief in the effect of drama in performance, reappears in his description of poetic image: 'Shall we be rid of the pride of intellect, of sedentary meditation, of emotion that leaves us when the book is closed or the picture seen no more; and live amid the thoughts than can go with us by steamboat and railway as once upon horseback, or camel-back, rediscovering, by our reintegration of the mind, ... the old abounding, nonchalent reverie?[81]

IV

Stage Production and the Greek Theatre Movement: W.B. Yeats's play The Resurrection and his versions of King Oedipus and Oedipus at Colonus

'What if Christ and Oedipus or, to shift the names, Saint Catherine of Genoa and Michael Angelo, are the two scales of a balance, the two butt-ends of a seesaw?'[1] Christ and Oedipus, the contrasting images in *A Vision*, were central figures in Yeats's theatre work in the late 1920s. Following the publication of *A Vision* in 1925, Yeats completed his versions of Sophocles' two plays of Oedipus. Designed for the main stage at the Abbey Theatre, *King Oedipus* was produced in 1926 and *Oedipus at Colonus* the following year. During that time Yeats wrote a play on the death of Christ based on his work with the Sophocles play but designed for the smaller Peacock Theatre, the Abbey's new experimental stage. Yeats's play *The Resurrection* was produced in the main stage in 1934. Those three productions were the culmination of Yeats's long involvement in two aspects of nonnaturalistic theatre — the relation between stage performance and audience in the Greek theatre, and the nature of the poetic and dramatic image produced in that type of theatre. Yeats shared those interests with a group of actors and producers, most notably Sybil Thorndike, Granville Barker, and Gilbert Murray, and one of the concerns of their early work, from 1900 to 1914, was a revival of Greek drama based on new archaeological theories of classical Greek theatre. Proscenium stages were converted to resemble Greek theatres, and a method of production was developed along the lines suggested by theories of the ritual origin of drama.

The Resurrection, based on those early experimental productions, illustrates Yeats's interest in the relation between performance and audience. His skill in combining the stage action of actors and chorus with the imaginative participation of the audience grew in part from his alterations of Sophocles' plays. Yeats's adaptations of the chorus in *King Oedipus* to fit the Abbey stage illustrates his contribution to methods of production and leads to a further consideration of the way drama reflects and shapes the interests of the audience. Yeats's views of the effect of the stage image and his theory of drama in performance were strikingly similar to Jane Harrison's. In light of those theories, Yeats's *Oedipus at Colonus* was both the presentation of a figure from classical drama and an invocation of Irish tradition.

The Greek theatre movement in England began in the 1880s with rediscoveries of Elizabethan and Greek theatre architecture.[2] The work of classicists and archaeologists was soon adapted to the modern stage by small amateur dramatic societies in the 1880s and 1890s. The architect and stage designer E. W. Godwin was among the first to base his work on the new theories (see Plate 22). When his son Gordon Craig began to design stage sets, he drew inspiration from the Greek and medieval theatre. Craig's favourite text was E. K. Chambers's *Medieval Stage* (1903), in which liturgical drama is considered as a development of church ritual shaped by the architecture of the cathedral.[3] Craig attached the same importance to architecture and thought the next development of drama would follow upon the demise of the proscenium stage. His system of folding screens, first used at the Abbey Theatre in 1911, acted as a practical alternative for poetic drama. Before his invention, as Craig explained in the 1910 Patent for the screens, there had been only two choices of stage design for poetic drama: 'scenery formed and painted so as to produce an illusion of the actual scene intended by the playwright, or using plain curtains as a background.'[4]

Plain curtains had at first offered the best solution for the conversion of proscenium stages for earlier forms of drama. In the 1880s William Poel developed a version of the Elizabethan stage by using an apron stage and dividing the proscenium stage with a curtain. With three acting areas he could produce the Elizabethan plays as a continuous action rather than a series of painted scenes. A less successful use of curtains was made by Granville Barker (one of Poel's actors) in his productions of Shakespeare (1912-1914). *The Winter's Tale* (1912) was performed on a stage divided by two parallel proscenium arches and extended over the orchestra. Though the arrangement allowed the same continuous action as Poel's settings, the production was controversial. As one spectator reported, 'Now there is a tendency among some neo-Shakespearian reformers to add Greek unity to the Renaissance variety of setting, by taking a lot of scenes, such as a Shakespearian play contains, and binding them together with curtains.'[5] Granville Barker, the reviewer continued, used his curtains incorrectly, in harmony merely with costumes or minor emotional motives: 'Thus, the first curtain, with its landscape and houses painted in the flat on a yellow ground, has no relation to the second curtain, with its composition in pinks, greens, yellows and blues. Nor has the zig-zag curtain any relation to those that preceded and followed it.'[6] The proper use of curtains should have been 'to express and sustain the predominant motive of the play. For instance, if the play is *Romeo and Juliet,* then the passionate love-motive would be seen running through all the lines and colours of the curtains.... Just as the Russian decorators have introduced the motive into the act-drop, curtains and background of the Russian Ballets, so a Shakespearian decorator here and there is seeking to introduce it to the Shakespearian curtain and screen scenes.'[7] Yeats followed closely the early productions of Poel, Craig and Granville Barker. His own theatre work was part of that movement, as he reminded his publisher in 1913. Yeats asked that a collection of his theatre criticism be published as soon as possible: 'Coming at this moment when people have in their memories the Reinhardt productions, the scenery and costumes of the Russian Ballet, the Barker productions of Shakespeare — all examples of the new decorative method — it would probably get considerable attention. It would contain the only serious criticism of the new craft of the Theatre. It is the exact moment for it.'[8]

Among the works Yeats cited to his publisher was Max Reinhardt's version of *Oedipus Rex.* Performed in London in

1912, it was possibly the most influential production of the Greek theatre movement. Reinhardt based his production on German theories of Greek theatre design which had been developed from conflicting archaeological discoveries. Had there been, as Vitruvius claimed, a large raised stage separating actors from chorus and spectators, or had there simply been a long step against the skene wall, with all performers using the orchestra space, distinguished only by costume and mask.'[9] The archaeological controversy closely affected changes in German theatre. Richard Wagner's work was, of course, based on the Greek theatre. In his view, the type of stage was crucial in determining the type of drama: "The form of a Shakespeare play would be as unintelligible to us as that of a Greek play without our knowledge of the stage necessities which shaped both the one and the other. Neither, though both contain poetry which is supreme poetry, took its form from poetry; neither is intelligible as poetic form.'[10] When Wagner's theatre at Bayreuth was completed, it soon became the model for the Greek movement. As Yeats wrote in 1901, 'Were our theatres of the shape of a half-closed fan, like Wagner's theatre, where the audience sit on seats that rise towards the broad end while the play is played at the narrow end, their pictures could be composed for eyes at a small number of points of view, instead of for eyes at many points of view, above and below and at the sides, and what is no better than a trade might become an art.'[11] A theatre where spectators are united by a common vantage point was difficult to achieve in the older buildings, where the stalls were separated from the stage by an orchestra pit. Wagner had called the pit a 'mystic gulf,' and he had designed the Bayreuth orchestra pit to fit below the stage level so that the music — 'the loam of universal feeling' — would complement rather than obscure the performance. 'In the Greek play,' he explained, 'the chorus appeared in the orchestra, that is, in the midst of the audience, while the personages, masked and heightened, were seen in a ghostly illusion of grandeur on the stage.'[12] Not until Max Reinhardt's productions in 1911 and 1912 could large audiences in London see that type of stage performance.

Reinhardt's *Oedipus Rex* radically altered the relation between performers and spectators. Gilbert Murray, who pre-

Stage Production and the Greek Theatre Movement

pared the English text, described the effect of the production:

> Vast audiences come to hear the *Oedipus* — audiences at any rate far greater than Mr. Granville Barker and I have ever gathered, except perhaps once; they sit enthralled for two hours of sheer tragedy, and I do not think many of them will forget that experience.[13]

Reinhardt had planned to restage his Berlin production of *Oedipus Rex* (see Plate 23), performed in a circus to an audience of five thousand,

> ... because that form of building is best suited to my requirements. The actors do really move among the audience, there playing out their little drama in the midst of their fellow-men, just as the great drama is played every day of our life on earth.[14]

After an unsuccessful attempt to use the Albert Hall, Reinhardt converted the interior of Covent Garden Theatre to recreate the effect of the Berlin production

> ... (T)he entire proscenium was fitted with a black screen representing the front of the palace of Oedipus. The centre of this screen was occupied by high, impressive brass doors, on either side of which there were three massive black columns supporting a grim portico. The orchestra well was covered by a black platform, with a piece projecting from the centre upon which the altar was placed. On either side of this 'apron' flights of steps led to the arena, or ball-room of the theatre. This floor formed a lower stage, and was built up in order to enable the spectator to realise that he was participating in the scene before him.[15]

As Reinhardt extended the acting area towards the audience, he also drew the audience towards the actors on stage. To make this arrangement possible,

> a space was cleared in front of the stage by removing rows of stalls, for the chorus and crowd to act in and mix with the spectators. The front row of the stalls was, in fact, in touch with the outer fringe of the crowd, while all the players made their entrances and exits through the audience at various points of the arena.[16]

The large chorus was a powerful connection between the spectators and performers. As one spectator described the supplication dance (see Plate 24),

> Perhaps the most artistic effect was that attained by the crowd and Oedipus. Oedipus stood on the rostrum calm and self-possessed. Beneath him surged

the infuriated mob, with outstretched arms, swelling up to him like a sea of angry emotions, and returning thence to the leader of the Chorus in response to his call. There on one side Oedipus stood like an intellectual pinnacle islanded in the billowing ocean of human beings; and there on the other side the Leader stood like the spirit of the Indefinite swayed to and fro by elemental passions.[17]

Reinhardt's production resembled Nietzsche's evocation of *The Birth of Tragedy* of a dramatic form based on 'the Dionysian chorus which ever anew discharges itself in an Appollinian world.'[18] His inspired description of an ancient Greek performance was the ideal of the Greek theatre movement:

The chorus is the 'ideal spectator' insofar as it is the only beholder, the beholder of the visionary world of the scene. A public of spectators as we know it was unknown to the Greeks: in their theatres the terraced structure of concentric arcs made it possible for everybody to actually *overlook* the whole world of culture around him and to imagine, in absorbed contemplation, that he himself was a chorist.

In the light of this insight we may call the chorus in its primitive form, in proto-tragedy, the mirror image in which the Dionysian man contemplates himself. This phenomenon is best made clear by imagining an actor who, being truly talented, sees the role he is supposed to play quite palpably before his eyes. The satyr chorus is, first of all, a vision of the Dionysian mass of spectators, just as the world of the stage, in turn, is a vision of this satyr chorus: the force of this vision is strong enough to make the eye insensitive and blind to the impression of 'reality', to the men of culture who occupy the rows of seats all around. The form of the Greek theatre recalls a lonely valley in the mountains: the architecture of the scene appears like a luminous cloud formation that the Bacchants swarming over the mountains behold from a height like the splendid frame in which the image of Dionysus is revealed to them.[19]

W. B. Yeats's play, *The Resurrection*, is a development of the early work of the Greek theatre movement. As playwright, theatre critic, producer and stage manager, Yeats gained the skill to compose a drama based on Christ's resurrection which was startling in concept and certainly powerfully effective for an Irish audience. The figure of Christ was one of the central images in *A Vision* (1925), published a few years before Yeats began work on the new play. The philosophical system of *A Vision*, based on the imagery of the double gyres and phases of the moon, is inherently dramatic.[20] As the gyres spin round, each point on the one spiral is matched by its opposite point on

Stage Production and the Greek Theatre Movement

the other. In terms of dramatic movement, each situation contains its own undoing. While the system of *A Vision* is dramatic, the figures, representing each phase resemble more the icons of a cathedral fresco, more design than movement:

> Oedipus lay upon the earth at the middle point between four sacred objects, was there washed as the dead are washed, and thereupon passed with Theseus to the wood's heart until amidst the sound of thunder earth opened, 'riven by love', and he sank down soul and body into the earth. I would have him balance Christ who, crucified standing up, went into the abstract sky soul and body, and I see him altogether separated from Plato's Athens, from all that talk of the Good and the One, from all that cabinet of perfection, an image from Homer's age.[21]

Yeats wrote the first draft of *The Resurrection* with the Abbey proscenium stage in mind: 'an ordinary stage scene in the mind's eye, curtained walls, a window and door at back, a curtained door at left.'[22] The scenario followed the iconographic design of *A Vision*. Christ, wrapped in grave clothes, meets a succession of dying gods — first Dionysus, then Buddha.

> Then Christ sees many persons coming. He asks 'Who are these', and is told 'Gods who have died for men'. He is about to kneel, but Buddha stops him. He answers 'I am still a man'. Buddha says 'Only the god who suffers lives, or only the act is divine — in that we put on divinity; now one, now another as the turning heavens decree.' They pass singing before him and bow as they pass. Their song is 'Why have you troubled me said Saul' enlarged to a stanza or chorus, and verses about the risen Christ. They pass out and the women pass out, all but three. Christ bursts out about the eternal sins of man, his vain suffering. Buddha, who alone of the men remains, says, 'Look, they kneel to you — Mary your mother, the other Maries, chief of all your worshippers.' Christ spreads out his arms. 'I am the life and the way.'[23]

In the final version this recognition belongs not to Christ but to a small group — a Greek, a Hebrew and a Syrian — who are guarding the disciplines from a Dionysian mob as they await news of Christ's crucifixion. The analogy between Christ and the other gods, originally depicted by an episodic structure, is suggested in the final version by the parallel between Christ's disciples and the Dionysian revellers. The Musicians' opening song introduces the analogy:

> I
> I saw a staring virgin stand
> Where holy Dionysus died,

Players and Painted Stage

> And tear the heart out of his side,
> And lay the heart upon her hand
> And bear that beating heart away;
> And then did all the Muses sing
> Of Magnus Annus at the spring,
> As though God's death were but a play.
>
> II
>
> Another Troy must rise and set,
> Another lineage feed the crow,
> Another Argo's painted prow
> Drive to a flashier bauble yet.
> The Roman Empire stood appalled:
> It dropped the reins of peace and war
> When that fierce virgin and her Star
> Out of the fabulous darkness called.   (579-580)

The disciples await Christ as the revellers await Dionysus, but there is yet a third parallel in the play. Yeats wrote the final version of *The Resurrection* for the new experimental Peacock Theatre at the Abbey. With an audience of only a hundred, closely connected with the stage by a long, low step, the Peacock could be used for a miniature version of the kind of production developed by the Greek theatre movement. Yeats devised the play so that the spectators, like the disciples and the revellers, would become part of the performance.

As the play begins, the Musicians sit on the long step. After their opening song, the Greek approaches the stage through the audience. Christ has been crucified, and the Greek brings word to the Hebrew that a Dionysian mob is approaching. The Hebrew faces the audience: 'I shall defend the narrow stairs between this and the street until I am killed, then you will take my place.' The stairs lead into the audience, now the street of the approaching mob.

The following dialogue further connects the audience with the stage performance. The Hebrew is satisfied to find the dead Christ merely human. As the two men stare out over the audience, the Greek laughs at the sight of Calvary and at the notion that Christ could have been anything but a pure spirit, a bodiless phantom.[24] The imaginary mob approaches and the Greek's words place the Dionysians in the midst of the audience. These revellers are mistaken, he insists, for they have taken their parts seriously, frenzied by a mere play:

Stage Production and the Greek Theatre Movement

> The Greek [*who is standing facing the audience, and looking out over their heads*]. It is the worshippers of Dionysus. They are under the window now. There is a group of women who carry upon their shoulders a bier with an image of the dead god upon it. No, they are not women. They are men dressed up as women. I have seen something like it in Alexandria. They are all silent, as if something were going to happen. My God! What a spectacle! In Alexandria a few men paint their lips vermilion. They imitate women that they may attain in worship a woman's self-abandonment. No great harm comes of it — but here! Come and look for yourself.
>
> The Hebrew. I will not look at such madmen.
>
> The Greek. Though the music has stopped, some men are still dancing, and some of the dancers have gashed themselves with knives, imagining themselves, I suppose, at once the god and the Titans that murdered him. A little further off, a man and a woman are coupling in the middle of the street. She thinks the surrender to some man the dance threw into her arms may bring her god back to life.... The crowd has parted to make way for a singer. It is a girl. No, not a girl; a boy from the theatre. I know him. He acts girls' parts. He is dressed as a girl, but his finger-nails are gilded and his wig is made of gilded cords. He looks like a statue cut out of some temple. I remember something of the kind in Alexandria. Three days after the full moon, a full moon in March, they sing the death of the god and pray for his resurrection.
>
> (585-586)

'What a spectacle' — the metaphor of theatre is carefully balanced. The audience watches the actors in a performance. The imaginary mob seems equally convinced of the performance, the incarnation of Dionysus.

The analogy between the audience and the Dionysians is developed in the following episodes. The Greek, dismissing the performance in the street as 'self-surrender and self-abandonment,' offers another explanation for the appearance of the god:

> [Man] copies their [the gods'] gestures and their acts. What seems their indifference is but their eternal possession of themselves. Man, too, remains separate. He does not surrender his soul. He keeps his privacy.
>
> (588)

His exclusion of the mob from his own group on stage disappears as the ecstatic self-abandonment is brought on stage. The Hebrew steps into the audience to help the Syrian:

> The Syrian. I am like a drunken man. I can hardly stand upon my feet. Something incredible has happened. I have run all the way.[25]
>
> (588)

He brings word to the disciples that Christ is missing from the tomb. To the Hebrew and the Greek, the news is heresy, similar to the mob's frenzied mime, that Christ could be both man and god. They hold him back from the inner room. The Hebrew and the Greek interpret his report in the light of their own beliefs, the dead man stolen, the god a pure spirit. The Syrian presses them:

> What matter if it contradicts all human knowledge? — another Argo seeks another fleece, another Troy is sacked.
>
> (590)
>
> ....
>
> What if there is always something that lies outside knowledge, outside order? What if at the moment when knowledge and order seem complete that something appears?
> [*He has begun to laugh.*   (591)

The Syrian's laughter further links the audience with events on stage. A mysterious presence, expressed first through laughter, moves from the audience to the stage:

> The Hebrew. Stop! He laughed when he saw Calvary through the window, and now you laugh.
> The Greek. He too has lost control of himself.
> The Hebrew. Stop, I tell you. [*Drums and rattles.*]
> The Syrian. But I am not laughing. It is the people out there who are laughing.
> The Hebrew. No, they are shaking rattles and beating drums.
> The Syrian. I thought they were laughing. How horrible!
> The Greek [*looking out over heads of audience*]. The worshippers of Dionysus are coming this way again.
>
> (591-592)

The shift of laughter prepares the audience for the entrance of Christ. As the Greek stares out into the audience,

> How they roll their painted eyes as the dance grows quicker and quicker. They are under the window. Why are they all suddenly motionless? Why are all those unseeing eyes turned upon this house? Is there anything strange about this house?
>
> (592)

Christ enters the room and the Greek crosses to him:

Stage Production and the Greek Theatre Movement

> There is nothing here but a phantom, it has no flesh and blood. Because I know the truth I am not afraid. Look, I will touch it. It may be hard under my hand like a statue — I have heard of such things — or my hand may pass through it — but there is no flesh and blood. [*He goes slowly up to the figure and passes his hand over its side.*] The heart of a phantom is beating! The heart of a phantom is beating! [*He screams. The figure of Christ crosses the stage and passes into the inner room.*]²⁶ (593)

In the final moments of the play, the dramatic action is gathered again into the iconographic design of *A Vision*, into image, epigram, lyric. The Greek touching the beating heart becomes, in the Syrian's words, the image of the doubting Thomas. The Greek recalls Heraclitus: 'God and man die each other's life, live each other's death.' The culmination of movement into image is repeated in the Musicians' final song:

> I
> In pity for man's darkening thought
> He walked that room and issued thence
> In Galilean turbulence;
> The Babylonian starlight brought
> A fabulous, formless darkness in;
> Odour of blood when Christ was slain
> Made all Platonic tolerance vain
> And vain all Doric discipline.
>
> II
> Everything that man esteems
> Endures a moment or a day:
> Love's pleasure frives his love away,
> The painter's brush consumes his dreams;
> The herald's cry, the soldier's tread
> Exhaust his glory and his might:
> Whatever flames upon the night
> Man's own resinous heart has fed. (594)

The complex rhythmic argument of the first stanza — Galilean turbulence, Babylonian starlight, Platonic tolerance vain, Doric discipline — becomes in the final stanza the more abrupt stresses, like a quickened drum beat, accompanying the final images — love's pleasure, painter's brush, herald's cry, soldier's tread. The stage action is figured again in the lyric.

> Whatever flames upon the night
> Man's own resinous heart has fed.

The Resurrection illustrates clearly Yeats's interest in the type of dramatic performance developed from the Greek theatre rather than the proscenium stage. His earlier dance plays, based in part on his collaboration with Gordon Craig and the Second Company (1909-1914) and in part on his adaptation of the Japanese Noh form (1912-1917), were developed from similar principles though intended for a small drawing-room audience and intimate performance. *The Resurrection* illustrates too the nature of the dramatic image Yeats intended to produce. It was as if Yeats's audience, denied the intercession of Nietzsche's visionary chorus, had come down into the orchestra to sustain the vision of the actor on stage. The nature of the dramatic image is at once an absorbing and illusive subject, depending as it must on the particulars of dramatic and scenic construction as well as the more speculative notions of imagination and memory. Both aspects of the dramatic image are represented in Yeats's work. His versions of Sophocles' Oedipus plays, adapted in the 1920s for the Abbey proscenium stage, illustrate the importance he attached to the composition of the heroic figure, while his theory of drama, with its close affinity to the works of Jane Harrison, sets out the long-ranging consequences he expected of the dramatic image.

Yeats's plans for *King Oedipus* and *Oedipus at Colonus* were begun in the early years of the Greek theatre movement.[27] In the winter of 1904, Yeats asked his theatre colleague, Gilbert Murray, to help with the translation. Murray discouraged him, suggesting instead a production — 'with a seditious innuendo'[28] — of *Prometheus, The Persae* or *Antigone*:

> I will not translate the Oedipus Rex for the Irish Theatre, because it is a play with nothing Irish about it: no religion, not one beautiful action, hardly a stroke of poetry. Even the good things that have to be done in order to make the plot work are done through mere loss of temper. The spiritual tragedy is never faced or understood: all the stress is laid on the mere external uncleanness. Sophocles no doubt did many bad things in his life. I would not try to shield him from just blame. But in this case I am sure, he was in a trance and his body was possessed by a series of devils — Sardou, the Lord Mayor of London, Aristotle, the Judicious Hooker, and all the editors of the *Spectator* from its inception to the present day. It has splendid acting qualities as an acting play, but all of the most English-French-German sort; it is all construction and no spirit.

Stage Production and the Greek Theatre Movement

> I am really distressed that the Censor objected to it. It ought to be played not perhaps at His Majesty's by Tree, but by Irving at the Lyceum, with a lecture before... and after. And a public dinner. With speeches, By Cabinet Ministers.[29]

Yeats made his own version of *Oedipus Rex*, finishing a rough draft of the dialogue by 1911. He hoped to produce the play in Gordon Craig's new scenery, but Craig's hesitations led to an indefinite postponement.[30] When Yeats returned to the play in the late 1920s, he recalled the confusion of those early years:

> When I first lectured in America... I heard at the University of Notre Dame that they had played *Oedipus the King*. That play was forbidden by the English censorship on the ground of its immorality; Oedipus commits incest; but in a Catholic university could perform it in America my own theatre could perform it in Ireland. Ireland had no censorship, and a successful performance might make her proud of her freedom, say even, perhaps, 'I have an old historical religion moulded to the body of man like an old suit of clothes, and am therefore free.'... When I got back to Dublin I found a young Greek scholar,... a manuscript translation of *Oedipus* too complicated in its syntax for the stage, bought Jebb's translation and a translation published at a few pence for dishonest schoolboys. Whenever I could not understand the precise thoughts behind the translator's half Latin, half Victorian dignity, I got a bald translation from my Greek scholar. I spoke out every sentence, very often from the stage, with one sole object, that the words should sound natural and fall in their natural order, that every sentence should be a spoken, not a written sentence. Then when I had finished the dialogue in the rough and was still shrinking at the greater labour of the choruses, the English censor withdrew his ban and I lost interest.[31]

Yeats's final version of *King Oedipus* was markedly different from Max Reinhardt's famous production. Gilbert Murray had agreed to translate the play for Reinhardt, and as we have seen, Covent Garden Theatre was converted into a large Greek theatre. Yeats adapted his version for the Abbey Theatre, constrained by a limited budget and small proscenium stage. His version transforms the tragedy of a community into that of the lone figure Oedipus, a modern 'tragic hero.' This transformation is most apparent in two instances, in the adaptation of the chorus to fit the Abbey orchestra pit, and in the restructuring of the final episode.

Choral presentation had always been a problem at the Abbey, and the Company had looked to London productions for a solution. John Millington Synge wrote in 1904 to Stephen

MacKenna, 'Did you see Murray's *Hypolitus* [sic] and if you did what did you make of their method of chorusing?'[32] Florence Farr, Murray's Chorus Leader, had taught them the method which she and Yeats called Cantilation, or Singing to the Psaltery.[33] Sybil Thorndike has described the experiments in subsequent productions of the *Hippolytus*:

> The chief trouble, as always in presenting Greek plays, was the management of the chorus both in speech and movement; and the correspondence between Murray and Archer at this period shows how much the matter was on both their minds. The tiny stage at the Court precluded the proper separation of the actors from the Chorus and any elaborate form of stylised formal movement; the choruses at first were spoken or chanted rather monotonously by single voices to the melancholy accompaniment of the Leader (Florence Farr) on a psaltery. In the later productions experiments were made with simple orchestral accompaniment and with trained choral speaking, and (at the Savoy, where there was more room) some formal choric movement. But no satisfactory solution of the problem was found.[34]

The Abbey Theatre had only a small, dark orchestra pit, and so it was necessary for the stage area to serve as both the orchestra and the raised stage of a Greek theatre (see Plate 25). Yeats reduced the chorus to a Leader and five men because, he wrote, 'This version of Sophocles' play was written for Dublin players, for Dublin liturgical singers, for a small auditorium, for a chorus that must stand stock still where the orchestra are accustomed to put their chairs.'[35] He adapted the chorus to 'preserve the mood while it rests the mind by change of attention,'[36] a technique he based on a Salvation Army meeting. As he explained in a 1931 BBC Belfast broadcast of the Abbey production,

> Probably the first thing that will seem to you very strange, very unlike anything seen on the English stage, is that every few minutes a number of persons who are called citizens of Thebes sing their comments upon the actors. I never understood the dramatic value of their singing, perhaps the sole reason for its existence from the point of view of a theatrical producer, until I attended a meeting of the Salvation Army in Dublin. They had hired the Abbey Theatre for a Sunday evening, and unnoticed by anybody I went to a little window high up above the stage platform among the pulleys and ropes that lower the stage scenes, and stood there listening. There were, I think, five sermons, all with a single idea — Christ's presence in the world — and between every sermon came a hymn. And I found that, rested by the change of attention made possible by the hymn, the change to a different kind of attention, I listened to the exposition of one idea taken up by speaker

Stage Production and the Greek Theatre Movement

after speaker without any sense on monotony. A Greek play, unlike a Shakespearian play, is the exposition of one idea; in the case of *King Oedipus*, fate closing in upon one man who is almost continuously on stage. There is no comic relief, no Polonius with his worldly wisdom and his absurdity, no gravedigger taking off, perhaps in accordance to an ancient stage tradition, innumerable waistcoats, no sub-plot, no Fortinbras with his filibustering army, but a chorus is there so that we may sit back and relax our strained attention. Not that we cease to listen, for the chorus is beautiful — past ages are called up before us, vast emotions are aroused — but our attention is no longer concentrated upon a single spot, a single man.[37]

In contrast with Max Reinhardt's chorus which retained the dramatic response of the original play, Yeats's chorus is more lyrical. Take for instance the fourth choral song, which follows upon the angry exchanges of Oedipus and Tiresias. The King has been accused of incest, murder and self-banishment, and in Gilbert Murray's translation, the chorus sings its suspicion and fear. Yeats's version removes the turn between strophe and antistrophe, the strong pull between suspicion and denial emphasized in Murray's summing up of the themes of each: *'They sing of the unknown murderer... And of the Prophet's strange accusation.'*[38]

> The Delphian rock has spoken out, now must a wicked mind,
> Planners of things I dare not speak and of this bloody wrack,
> Pray for feet that are as fast as the four hoofs of the wind:
> Cloudy Parnassus and the Fates thunder at his back.
>
> That sacred crossing-place of the lines upon Parnassus' head,
> Lines that have run through North and South, and run through West and East,
> That navel of the world bids all men search the mountain wood,
> That solitary cavern, till they have found that infamous beast.
>
> (488)

This change in the relation between the King and the Thebans — in Yeats's version, an action on stage followed by comment and reflection from the chorus in the small orchestra pit — is again apparent in the final episode, from the entrance of the blinded Oedipus. Yeats omits about half the dialogue in which Oedipus's self-revulsion is mirrored by the horror of the Thebans'. In the original play, Oedipus recounts at length his past deeds, speaking now from belief rather than suspicion and accusation. The Thebans' response is one of revulsion: 'Wretched alike for thy fortune and thy sense thereof, would that I

Players and Painted Stage

had never so much as known thee.'[39] Yeats, in reducing this doubled revulsion of King and citizens, has created instead a dramatic movement which culminates in the lone figure of Oedipus surrounded by his weeping daughter and Creon. The isolation of Oedipus is figured again in the single actor, the Chorus Leader, who addresses the final song to the Abbey audience.[40]

> Make way for Oedipus. All people said,
> 'That is a fortunate man';
> And now what storms are beating on his head!
> Call no man fortunate that is not dead.
> The dead are free from pain. (517)

Yeats's subsequent version of *Oedipus at Colonus* for the Abbey in 1927 followed the same revision — a reduction of the role of the chorus serving in effect to isolate and enhance the main figure.[41] A successful production, *Oedipus at Colonus* was at the same time a full dramatic presentation of one of the central images in Yeats's own work — the daemonic old beggarman. The poems in *The Tower*, published after Yeats's work with the Oedipus productions, present a similar figure of an old man feeble of body but powerful of spirit.

> An aged man is but a paltry thing,
> A tattered coat upon a stick, unless
> Soul clap its hands and sing, and louder sing
> For every tatter in its mortal dress
>   'Sailing to Byzantium'
>
> What shall I do with this absurdity —
> O heart, O troubled heart — this caricature,
> Decrepit age that has been tied to me
> As to a dog's tail?
>   Never had I more
> Excited, passionate, fantastical
> Imagination, nor an ear and eye
> That more expected the impossible —
>   'The Tower'[42]

This reversal from weakness to power resembles of course the pattern of the double gyres in *A Vision*, of life-in-death and death-in-life. Dramatically depicted in *Oedipus at Colonus*, the pattern is the basis of Yeats's theory of the origin of the image:

Stage Production and the Greek Theatre Movement

> ... I seek an image, not a book.
>
> ....
>
> I call to the mysterious one who yet
> Shall walk the wet sands by the edge of the stream
> And look most like me, being indeed my double,
> And prove of all imaginable things
> The most unlike, being my anti-self,
> And...   disclose
> All that I seek...
>   'Ego Dominus Tuus'[43]

Yeats called the anti-self 'the hollow image of fulfilled desire' and in *Per Amica Silentia Lunae* (1917) he described what he considered the transformation of emotion into image:

> But the passions, when we know that they cannot find fulfilment, become vision; and a vision, whether we wake or sleep, prolongs its power by rhythm and pattern, the wheel where the world is butterfly. We need no protection, but it does, for if we become interested in ourselves, in our own lives, we pass out of the vision. Whether it is we or the vision that create the pattern, who set the wheel turning, it is hard to say, but certainly we have a hundred ways of keeping it near us: we select our images from past times.[44]

Yeats's theory of the image bears comparison with that of Jane Harrison, inspired theorist of the early Greek theatre movement and member of the so-called Cambridge school of classical anthropology.[45] Her view of the origin of the image is remarkably similar to Yeats's anti-self:

> We have seen already that out of the space between an impulse and a reaction there arises an idea or 'presentation.' A 'presentation' is, indeed, it would seem, in its final analysis, only a delayed, intensified desire — a desire of which the active satisfaction is blocked, and which runs over into a 'presentation'. An image conceived 'presented,' what we call an *idea* is, as it were, an act prefigured.[46]

Basing her work on archaeological finds, Jane Harrison argued against the view that ritual was the debased form of myth. Her interest lay in the relation between emotion and dramatic or religious performance. She reversed the accepted view and suggested instead that myth was shaped from ritual. As she wrote in *Ancient Art and Ritual* (1914),

> Ritual... involves *imitation*, but does not arise out of it. It desires to recreate an emotion, not to reproduce an object.[47]

Underlying the ritual was an impulse 'to utter, to give out a strongly felt emotion or desire by representing, by making or doing or enriching the object or act desired.'[48] An image, then, was for both Yeats and Jane Harrison a representation of recurrent cycles or rhythms. As she wrote,

> Had there been no periodic festivals, personification might long have halted. But it is easy to see that a recurrent *per*ception helps to form a permanent abstract *con*ception. The different actual recurrent May Kings and 'Deaths', *because they recur*, get a sort of permanent life of their own and become beings apart. In this way a conception, a kind of *daimon*, or spirit, is fashioned, who dies and lives again in a perpetual cycle. The periodic festival begets a kind of not immortal, but perennial god.[49]

Jane Harrison supported her argument with Alfred North Whitehead's view that the 'whole life of Nature is dominated by the existence of periodic events.'[50] Yeats called those periodic events the 'hidden laws of the world,' which he felt were best depicted by 'wavering, meditative, organic rhythms.'[51] In 'Discoveries' (1906), he suggested that

> The end of art is the ecstasy awakened by the presence before an ever-changing mind of what is permanent in the world, or by the arousing of that mind itself into the very delicate and fastidious mood habitual with it when it is seeking those permanent and recurring things.[52]

The idea was further developed in *Per Amica Silentia Lunae* (1917):

> If all our mental images no less than apparitions (and I see no reason to distinguish) are forms existing in the general vehicle of *Anima Mundi*, and mirrored in our particular vehicle, many crooked things are made straight. I am persuaded that a logical process, or a series of related images, has body and period, and I think of *Anima Mundi* as a great pool or garden where it moves through its allotted growth like a great water-plant or fragrantly branches in the air.[53]

The Resurrection, King Oedipus, and *Oedipus at Colonus* were the culmination of Yeats's long interest in the adaptation of the Greek theatre to the modern stage. His motives were partly political, as in his early Abbey plays where issues of nascent Irish nationalism were represented by heroic characters from Irish legend. Though he thought Irish audiences would benefit from a knowledge of European classical drama, he was not guided by a narrow antiquarianism:

Stage Production and the Greek Theatre Movement

When I prepared 'Oedipus at Colonus' for the Abbey stage I saw that the wood of the Furies in the opening scene was any Irish haunted wood. No passing beggar or fiddler or benighted countryman has ever trembled or been awe-struck by nymph-haunted or Fury-haunted wood described in Roman poetry. Roman poetry is founded upon documents, not upon beliefs.[54]

In a 1931 BBC Belfast broadcast of *King Oedipus*, Yeats compared the play with *King Lear*, produced at the Abbey in 1928 with much the same cast:

> In the first play,... Oedipus brings upon himself the curse of the gods because of an involuntary sin, but in the second play he wanders an outcast from road to road, a blind old man, attended and protected by his two daughters as Lear was protected by Cordelia. So great has been his suffering that the gods have come over to his side and those that he curses perish and those that he blesses prosper.[55]

In those productions, as in *The Resurrection*, Yeats saw the dramatic images of the double gyres, the reversal from extreme misfortune to daemonic power. Thirty years before, he had suggested that

> It is indeed only those things which seem useless or very feeble that have any power, and all those things that seem useful or strong, armies, moving wheels, modes of architecture, modes of government, speculations of the reason, would have been a little different if some mind long ago had not given itself to some emotion... and shaped sounds or colours or forms, or all of these, into a musical relation, that their emotion might live in other minds.... I am certainly never sure, when I hear of some war, or of some religious excitement, or of some new manufacture, or of anything else that fills the ear of the world, that it has not all happened because of something that a boy piped in Thessaly. I remember once telling a seeress to ask one among the gods who, as she believed, were standing about her in their symbolic bodies, what would come of a charming but seeming trivial labour of a friend, and the form answering, 'the devastation of peoples and the overwhelming of cities.[56]

In *A Vision*, the major image of the power of the 'useless and very feeble' is the old man Oedipus:

> He knew nothing but his mind, and yet because he spoke that mind fate possessed it and kingdoms changed according to his blessing and his cursing.[57]

In the BBC broadcast Yeats placed Oedipus at the centre of contemporary Ireland. For an audience living through the turbulent events of the Easter Uprising, the Troubles and the

Civil War, Oedipus could be the image of intensity in the midst of disaster, pointing back to the 'permanent and recurring' Irish versions. The old man Oedipus was, in Yeats's words,

> the representative of human genius. We think perhaps of Jonathan Swift, hating himself first of all and then mankind, until suffering had made him half divine. And then perhaps by a strange freak of imagination we think of our blind Gaelic poet Raftery wandering with his blessings and his cursings from road to road.[58]

Gordon Craig's wood engraving, 'In Italy: Design for a Scene,' 1907.

Gordon Craig's wood engraving, 'Hamlet: An Actor', 1912, like Septimus in W. B. Yeats's The Player Queen: *'My breast-feathers thrust out and my white wings buoyed up with divinity.'*

'Hamlet and Daemon', one of a series of Gordon Craig's wood engravings included in an exhibition of his stage designs, arranged by W. B. Yeats, Dublin, 1913.

A photograph of Gordon Craig's model stage design for Stanislavski's production of Hamlet, *Moscow Art Theatre, 1911.*

Gordon Craig's wood engraving, 'Troy Burning', 1908, illustrating an arrangement of Craig's screens with expressive side lighting.

Gordon Craig's father, the architect E.W. Godwin, incorporated contemporary archaeological discoveries of classical Greek theatres in his stage set for Helen of Troy, Henglers Circus, London 1886.

Max Reinhardt's production of Sophocles' Oedipus Rex, which radically altered the relation between performers and spectators, was performed in the Schumann Circus to an audience of five thousand. Gouache by Emil Orlik, Berlin, 1910.

Max Reinhardt's London production of Oedipus Rex, Covent Garden 1912, for which the theatre was adapted to resemble a Greek theatre by the modification of the proscenium stage and the removal of the front stalls to make room for the Chorus.

W. B. Yeats's version of King Oedipus *was designed for the Abbey Theatre's small stage and small orchestra pit, shown in this view from the circle of another play in rehearsal.*

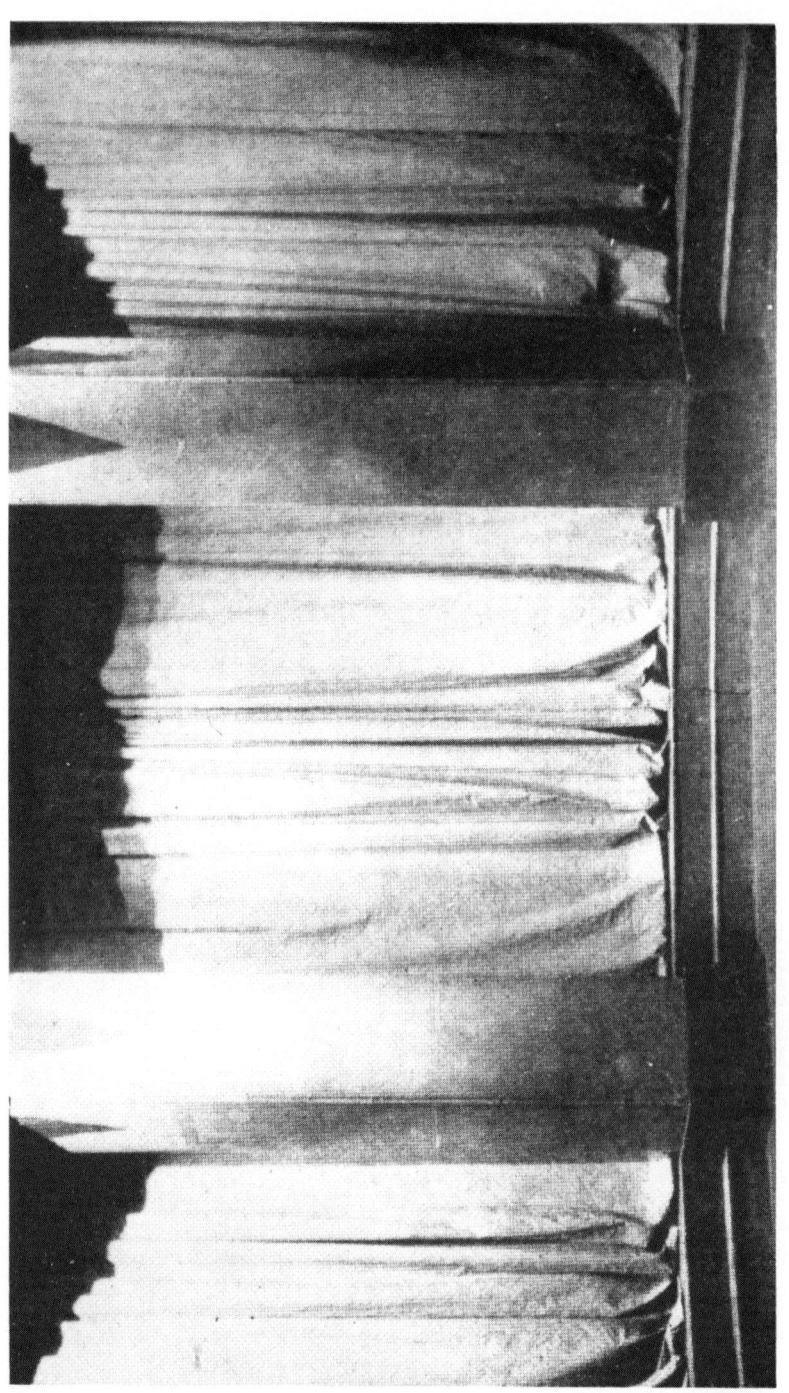

The stage set for the production of W. B. Yeats's version of King Oedipus *at the Abbey Theatre, 1926, included elements of the classical Greek theatre.*

The Festival Theatre, Cambridge, was the first English playhouse with a permanent stage based on the classical Greek theatre. The apron stage extending beyond the proscenium and the long front step can be seen in this photograph of the 1930 production of Antigone. The influence of Gordon Craig appears in the use of columns, ramps and steps to suggest the theme of the play.

D. Travers Smith's backcloth with a decorative pattern of the central image of waves for the 1929 London and Dublin productions of W. B. Yeats's Fighting the Waves. (See Plate 29).

Cuchulain's opening dance with the wave dancers, pupils of Ninette de Valois' Abbey School of Ballet, in the 1929 Abbey Theatre production of W. B. Yeats's Fighting the Waves. (See Plate 28).

The Mask of Fand, worn by Ninette de Valois in W. B. Yeats's Fighting the Waves, *London and Dublin 1929, designed by Hildo Krop for the 1922 Amsterdam production of* The Only Jealousy of Emer. *(See Plate 16).*

The masks and costumes for the King, Queen and Stroller in two Dublin productions of W. B. Yeats's The King of the Great Clock Tower. *Above, at the Abbey Theatre, Dublin, 1934: below, at the Gate Theatre, Dublin, 1942.*

The Mercury Theatre, London, where a number of avant garde *productions of ballet and poetical drama were produced in the 1930's. Though Yeats's plan to produce several of his plays at the Mercury Theatre was not realised, he praised the first London production there of T. S. Eliot's* Murder in the Cathedral *and recognised in the work of the Mercury Theatre and in its audiences the type of theatre for which he had worked.*

V

The New Dance Drama: Yeats's Last Dance Plays

'We have ceased to be spectators,' the stage designer Adolphe Appia wrote in 1929. In a summary of recent innovations in the theatre, he used an image recalling the Greek theatre movement: 'We have left our chairs.... We break the barriers asunder, surmount in a stride the steps that separate us from the stage, descend unflinchingly into the arena.'[1] Appia's view of the new theatre as a celebration of the *'living* reality,' 'the actor's living body,'[2] is an apt description of Yeats's last group of dance plays. Based on the form developed in *Four Plays for Dancers*, these plays were a response to a new audience and a new Irish theme. In 1930, Yeats compared his early work at the Abbey with contemporary developments: 'I wanted a theatre where the greatest passions and all the permanent interests of men might be displayed that we might find them not alone over a book but, as I have said again and again, lover by lover, friend by friend. All I wanted was impossible, and I wore out my youth in its pursuit, but now I know it is the mystery to come.'[3]

The inspiration for the new group of dance plays was, once again, a revival of *On Baile's Strand.* During the Abbey production of *King Oedipus* Yeats heard of the revival: 'They are playing my *Baile's Strand* at Cambridge from Jan 31 to Feb 5. The fool and blind man masked, and elaborate dancing of the witches and strange lighting.'[4] The Festival Theatre, Cambridge, was the first English playhouse to use a permanent stage similar to the conversions used for Greek tragedy.[5] (See Plate 27.) With a greatly reduced proscenium, the acting area was extended by an apron stage, ending in a long step. The stage settings, in the manner of Craig and Appia, were arrangements of cubes, cylinders, and steps suggesting the theme of the production.⁶ Yeats was delighted by the revival of *On Baile's Strand*, a play long associated with experimental stage performances. What especially caught his attention was the Irish dancer Ninette de Valois, a member of Diaghilev's Russian Ballet. She has described their meeting and his invitation to work in Dublin:

It is the year 1927 and I am sitting in the dark vestibule of the Festival Theatre in Cambridge. I am listening to a rich Irish voice that seems to intone a request that I should come to Dublin and produce for the Abbey Theatre. The voice belongs to William Butler Yeats, who has just witnessed a verse play of Gordon Bottomley's and some dance creations of my own.... It would seem that if I should return to Ireland at his impressive bidding (made to me in a light so dim that the speaker's features were not clear) I would work among those people whose efforts to establish the Irish Theatre were in progress at the time that I struggled with an Irish jig in a farmhouse at the foot of the Wicklow Hills.

The mind of Yeats was made up; he would have a small school of Ballet at the Abbey and I would send over a teacher. I would visit Dublin every three months and produce his *Plays for Dancers* and perform in them myself; thus, he said, the poetic drama of Ireland would live again and take its rightful place in the Nation's own Theatre, and the oblivion imposed on it by the popularity of peasant drama would become a thing of the past.⁷

Yeats planned a series of dance plays for Ninette de Valois' Abbey School of Ballet; 'There will be masks and all singing within the range of the speaking voice — for all my old theories are dogmas it seems of the new school.'⁸ His plans included a trilogy of *At the Hawk's Well, On Baile's Strand,* and *Fighting the Waves,* a new version of *The Only Jealousy of Emer* written for Ninette de Valois. In the late 1920s, *At the Hawk's Well* was produced with Ninette de Valois, as the hawk guardian, in Michio Itoh's costume from the 1916 production (see Plate 14).⁹ Her most exciting performance was in *Fighting the Waves,* produced in London and Dublin in 1929, the year Appia praised the growth of theatre based on 'dance and living statuary.'¹⁰ Ninette de Valois has mentioned the intense vitality and weight of character of her mask, designed by Hildo Krop for the 1922 Amsterdam production of *The Only Jealousy of Emer* (see Plate 30).¹¹ Yeats's adaptation of *The Only Jealousy of Emer* was directed towards simplifying the plot and strengthening the significance of her dance:

The Woman of Sidhe, Fand, moves round the crouching Ghost of Cuchulain

The New Dance Drama

at front of stage in a dance that grows gradually quicker as he awakes. At moments she may drop her hair upon his head, but she does not kiss him. She is accompanied by string and flute and drum. Her mask and clothes must suggest gold or bronze or brass and silver, so that she seems more an idol than a human being. This suggestion may be repeated in her movements. Her hair, too, must keep the metallic suggestion. The object of the dance is that having awakened Cuchulain he will follow Fand out; probably he will seek a kiss and the kiss will be withheld.[12]

As in the Japanese Noh performance, the Abbey production of *Fighting the Waves* was built upon a single image, 'a mask with the silver glitter of a fish,' 'a dance with an eddy like that of water,' and 'music that suggested, not the vagueness, but the rhythm of the sea.'[13] This controlling image appeared on the backdrop (Plate 28) as a decorative pattern of waves and was repeated in the movement of the wave dancers, acting as a frame for the two new dances. Cuchulain's opening dance (Plate 29) represents the final episode in *On Baile's Strand*, linking it with the last play of the trilogy:

Musicians and speaker off stage. There is a curtain with a wave pattern. A man wearing the Cuchulain mask enters from one side with sword and shield. He dances a dance which represents a man fighting the waves. The waves may be represented by other dancers: in his frenzy he supposes the waves to be his enemies: gradually he sinks down as if overcome, then fixes his eyes with a cataleptic stare upon some imaginary distant object. The stage becomes dark, and when the light returns it is empty. The Musicians enter. Two stand one on either side of the curtain, singing.[14]

After the Musicians' final song, Fand dances before the same backdrop. Like the central image of the seashore in *The Only Jealousy of Emer*, the decorative pattern of waves and the accompanying wave dancers suggest a similarity between Fand's bitterness and Cuchulain's despair at fighting the waves:

The Musicians return to their places. Fand, the Woman of the Sidhe, enters and dances a dance which expresses her despair for the loss of Cuchulain. As before there may be other dancers who represent the waves. It is called, in order to balance the first dance, 'Fand mourns among the waves.' It is essentially a dance which symbolises, like water in the fortune-telling books, bitterness. As she takes her final pose of despair the Curtain falls.[15]

The Abbey production encouraged the new company of actors and dancers. As Yeats wrote, 'My *Fighting the Waves* has been my greatest success of the stage since *Kathleen-ni-Houlihan*, and its production was a great event here, the politicians and the governor general and the American minister present — the masks by the Dutchman Krop magnificent and Antheil's music. Everyone here is as convinced as I am that I have discovered a new form by this combination of dance, speech and music.... The theatre was packed night after night, so the play will be revived.'[16]

During the next few years, the group established itself as a complement to the Abbey's naturalistic drama, much as Yeats's second company had done before the war. In the autumn of 1931, *The Cat and the Moon* was revived and *The Dreaming of the Bones* at last produced. A series of Sunday evening entertainments — 'Mainly ballet: the Abbey Directors' Sunday entertainments' — was organized to keep the audience together during the Abbey Company's American tour.[17] Yeats travelled with the company, the last tour he made. The lectures he prepared gave him a contemporary political theme that led in turn to a new dance play for Ninette de Valois — *The King of the Great Clock Tower,* 1934.

The Abbey tour was planned to give a comprehensive picture of modern Ireland. The Abbey players, Yeats explained in his BBC Belfast radio talk for *King Oedipus*, would take

> the Abbey plays all over the United States as far west as California, as far south as Texas. They want to show our plays to everybody, but are particularly anxious to show them to our own people and to the children of our own people. We are but four and a half millions here in Ireland, but there must be thirty million of us scattered through the world, of whom a portion are still ready to share our imagination and our discoveries. We are sending them a vision of the new Ireland, so full of curiosity, so full of self-criticism; our new satirical comedy, sometimes so tolerant, sometimes so bitter in its merriment.[18]

Yeats wanted to set out 'the origin of what seems to be the most unique and strange in our Irish excitement.' In 'Modern Ireland, an Address to American Audiences,' he spoke of three periods that had shaped the Irish character:

> The modern Irish nation began when at the end of the seventeenth century the victorious Protestant governing class quarrelled with England about the

The New Dance Drama

> wool trade. In 1705 or 6 Irish intellect declared its separate identity when Berkeley defined the Whig philosophy of Locke and Newton and wrote after his definition 'We Irish do not think so.' Irishmen of the new sort had been helped into power by sceptics and deists, but they were neither. Swift was their De Valera, their first turbulent self-assertion. Flinders Petrie would probably say the mingling of races, of Norman and Gael and Scot, were at last complete. The second formative moment came at the close of the eighteenth century. The Irish peasantry, who had obeyed now this master now that, began under the influence of the French revolution to assert their will and in the process discovered constitutional agitation and democratic Catholicism. At the close of the nineteenth century came the third moment. I saw it begin almost exactly forty years ago on a stormy autumn morning.
>
> I stood on Kingstown Pier, now Dun Laoghaire pier, a little after six, awaiting the mail boat. I was there to meet a friend and it was accident that I saw the arrival of Parnell's body.[19]

Yeats later published the lecture in a volume of commentary, poems, and *The King of the Great Clock Tower*. One passage in particular acts as a key to the structure of the new dance play:

> When lecturing in America I spoke of Four Bells, four deep tragic notes, equally divided in time, so symbolising the war that ended in the Flight of the Earls; the Battle of the Boyne; the coming of French influence among our peasants; the beginning of our own age; events that closed the sixteenth, seventeenth, eighteenth and nineteenth centuries. My historical knowledge, such as it is, begins with the 'Second Bell.'[20]

The King of the Great Clock Tower, dedicated to Ninette de Valois, represents the last of the 'Four Bells,' heralding an Ireland that was 'passing through a phase of self-conscious violence.'[21] The Queen dances with the severed head, accompanied by the Musicians' song, 'A slow low note and an iron bell.' Yeats recognized the same mood in Joyce's *Ulysses*, O'Casey's *The Plough and the Stars* and O'Flaherty's novels:

> Something new and terrible had come in Ireland, the mood of the mystic victim. For a generation speeches, commemorations led before men's minds the martyrs for the national cause, all the more popular national songs were in their praise; not one of them, not Lord Edward, nor Wolfe Tone, was the victim. They had served their cause and met their deaths, but they had not deliberately sought suffering.... Parnell had been the victim, the nation the priest, but now men were both priest and victim — they offered the nation a terrible way out [of] humiliation and self-destruction.[22]

Yeats recalled the description of an Irish Republican Army

leader who 'has a passion for suffering; he is always compelling people to persecute him.'[23] The 1916 uprising, Yeats suggested, had originated in part from a similar motive: 'Pearse is going through Ireland preaching the blood sacrifice —he says blood must be shed in every generation.' The concluding image of the lecture anticipates the sudden shift of emotion in the dance of *The King of the Great Clock Tower*:

> When I meet English and American writers, I find them toiling with great sincerity to discover through philosophy and criticism perfect and novel forms, but though discovery helps when the theme is found, it cannot giv;e the theme. When I would represent the finding of a theme, I think of a strange Eastern tale, of the Japanese boy who ran screaming from an abbot who had cut off his fingers, then, standing and looking back, suddenly attained Nirvana. The poetic theme is found, like sanctity, through desire and humiliation.[24]

This shift from horror to fascination is depicted in the tale of the King, Queen, and Stroller,[25] and suggested by the stage setting:

> When the curtains are parted one sees to the left the King and Queen upon two thrones, which may be two cubes. There should be two cubes upon the opposite side to balance them. The background may be a curtain hung in a semicircle, or a semicircle of one-foot Craig screens.
>
> (364)

When the Queen orders the Stroller beheaded, the King places the severed head 'upon the cubical throne to the right nearest audience.' The Queen's final dance expresses the change of power:

> When the song is finished, the dance begins again, the Clock strikes. The strokes are represented by blows on a gong struck by Second Attendant. The Queen dances to the sound, and at the last stroke presses her lips to the lips of the head. The King has risen and drawn his sword. The Queen lays the head upon her breast, and fixes her eyes upon him. He appears about to strike, but kneels, laying the sword at her feet. The two Attendants rise singing, and slowly close the inner curtains.
>
> (640)

Yeats's sense of the new 'mood of the mystic victim' in Ireland is here expressed in a dance he saw as part of an earlier tradition. In the Abbey programme notes he drew attention to Oscar Wilde's *Salome*, borrowed from Heine, dancing in Hell

The New Dance Drama

with the head of John the Baptist, and the old 'celebration of the Mother Goddess and her slain god, enacted probably at a full moon in March at the opening of the new year. In an Irish form of perhaps the same symbol there is no dance, but the head of a slain lover singing to his mistress. I have combined song and dance.'[26] In the final moments of the play both the stage set and the Musicians' ballad emphasize the central role of the dance. The Musicians draw open a curtain with a 'stencilled pattern of dancers':

> First Attendant. O, but I saw a solemn sight:
> *Said the rambling, shambling, travelling-man;*
> Castle Dargan's ruin all lit,
> Lovely ladies dancing in it.
>
> Second Attendant. What though they danced! Those days are gone,
> *Said the wicked, crooked, hawthorn tree;*
> Lovely lady or gallant man
> Are blown cold dust or a bit of bone.
>
> First Attendant. O, what is life but a mouthful of air?
> *Said the rambling, shambling, travelling-man;*
> Yet all the lovely things that were
> Live, for I saw them dancing there.   (640)

During the last verse, the Queen moves towards the audience, joining the stage movement with the images of the ballad:

> [*The Queen has come down stage and now stands framed in the half-closed curtains.*
>
> Second Attendant. Nobody knows what may befall,
> *Said the wicked, crooked, hawthorn tree.*
> I have stood so long by a gap in the wall
> Maybe I shall not die at all.   (641)

The King of the Great Clock Tower was produced with *The Resurrection* at the Abbey in 1934. (See Plate 31.) 'It would be impossible to overpraise the beauty of these productions,' the *Sunday Times* reviewer wrote.' ... An evening in the Abbey this week is a tonic to an Irishman who is inclined to be depressed about the fututre of his country.'[27] Ninette de Valois' dance of the Queen, together with her previous dances as the woman of the Sidhe and the hawk guardian, must have seemed to Yeats a fulfilment of his early work. In a note to 'The Hosting of the Sidhe' (1899), he had placed the Irish image within an older tradition: the Sidhe 'still ride the country as of old. Sidhe is also Gaelic for wind, and certainly the Sidhe have much to do with the wind. They journey in whirling wind, the winds that were called the dance of the daughters of Herodias in the Middle Ages, Herodias doubtless taking the place of some old goddess.'[28] With Ninette de Valois' dances in mind, Yeats revised *The King of the Great Clock Tower* after the Abbey production. The King was omitted, to emphasize 'the old ritual of the year: the mother goddess and the slain god.'[29] The new play, *A Full Moon in March*, was a dramatisation of the central image in 'Crazy Jane Grown Old Looks at the Dancers,' the close resemblance of love and loathing:

> I found that ivory image there
> Dancing with her chosen youth,
> But when he would her coal-black hair
> As though to strangle her, no scream
> Or bodily movement did I dare,
> Eyes under eyelids did so gleam;
> *Love is like the lion's tooth.*
>
> When she, and though some say she played
> I said that she had danced heart's truth,
> Drew a knife to strike him dead,
> I could but leave him to his fate;
> For no matter what is said
> They had all that had their hate;
> *Love is like the lion's tooth.*
>
> Did he die or did she die?
> Seemed to die or died they both?
> God be with the times when I
> Cared not a traneen for what chanced
> So that I had the limbs to try
> Such a dance as there was danced —
> *Love is like the lion's tooth.*

In *Fighting the Waves, The King of the Great Clock Tower*, and *A Full Moon in March*, Yeats adapted earlier dramatic work for a new dancer and a new political theme. Students of Yeats's last plays have drawn attention to the continuity of imagery, based in part on Yeats's lifelong study of neo-Platonic tradition.[30] It is also important to consider what greatly encouraged Yeats at the time — the new theatres and audiences. The Peacock Theatre, where *Fighting the Waves*,

The New Dance Drama

The Dreaming of the Bones, The Resurrection, and *The King of the Great Clock Tower* were first produced, and the Festival Theatre, Cambridge, where Yeats met Ninette de Valois, had been established in the 1920s, long after the experiments with Gordon Craig's screens and drawing room performances. The growth of interest in nonnaturalistic drama and the proliferation of the small arts theatres offered Yeats new opportunities. As he wrote in 1930, 'I disliked the isolation of the work of art. I wished through the drama, through a commingling of verse and dance, through singing that was also speech, through what I called the applied arts of literature, to plunge it back into social life.'[31]

The growth of interest in nonnaturalistic drama occurred both in Ireland and in England. In the late 1920s, an Irish amateur theatre movement began as part of the Irish Free State's revival of an ancient Gaelic competition, Aonachy Tailteann.[32] Those productions, held in the Abbey's Peacock Theatre, helped to build audiences for Ninette de Valois' Abbey School of Ballet and Yeats's dance plays. The interest of the new audiences differed from those who had supported the prewar experimental drama. Ashley Dukes, a major figure in the London theatre in the early 1930s, described the change in interest: 'Admittedly the theatre has changed very much since those (pre-war) days; and the common or critical explanation is that the dramatists have made the difference. Indeed those who interpret theatre in terms of drama alone imagine no other explanation... but we can say with certainty that the interest of the present English stage is *not* focused upon its playwrights, as it was twenty years ago. And that is the principle change in outlook.'[33]

Ashley Dukes's Mercury Theatre was an important focus for the pioneering work of the early 1930s. Dukes set up the Mercury for a new ballet company directed by his wife, Marie Rambert, and in 1933 he extended the programme to include dramatic productions. He thought the small theatre offered what the cinema and large commercial theatres lacked:

I would like to come back to the subject of the small professional art theatre, which has existed in many European cities in the last twenty years and may yet find a permanent home in London and New York. To my mind this sort of playhouse is one of the chief theatrical hopes, because it is the only sort of playhouse that can be indifferent equally to the demands of the large-scale theatre and the film studio. Larger and more impressive theatres will continue to exist, but this one should be regarded as the theatre proper, the theatre determined to keep theatre alive. It is the only sort of playhouse today that can possibly attract a cultivated audience, because it goes back to an Elizabethan simplicity of style. Also it is better to struggle with the help of a cultivated audience in a side street than to flourish on a main street with the aid of the movie millions.[34]

As the Mercury Theatre gained supporters, Ashley Dukes called for an end to the misleading notion of a general 'public' or 'public taste.' Twenty years earlier Yeats had written his first dance plays with the hope of building an audience interested in the same intellectual tradition. Now Ashley Dukes had the benefit of audiences drawn from the previous seasons of ballet: 'Of all London audiences, the most selective was that of Diaghilev's Russian Ballet, for it gave him crowded houses for four or five weeks of each year... and a great part of its members took no interest in any other kind of theatre at all.... It was interesting therefore to see how many of this large and faithful band would be captured by the Camargo Society, a ballet-producing organization on the lines of the Stage Society.'[35] In 1930, Ninette de Valois became a choreographer for the Camargo Society, producing a new form of dance based on her work at the Festival Theatre, Cambridge, and the Abbey. The close interplay between drama and ballet must surely have played a fundamental part in the work she and Marie Rambert did with the Sadler's Wells Company and the Ballet Rambert:

No choreographer is better at telling a story and creating characters. Ninette de Valois' two finest characterizations, Satan in Job and Mister O'Reilly in *The Prospect Before Us*, belong to the larger world of the theatre rather than to the conventionalized world of the ballet. They are not figures; they are human beings. Their ancestors are not the characters from old ballets; they are in the direct line of descent from the creations of the English novelists and dramatists. Even when in a ballet such as *Checkmate* Ninette de Valois' subject is superficially an abstract one, she gives humanity to her symbols. The Black and Red Queens, the Knights, the old Red King, are individuals who feel intensely, so that the ballet is full of the excitement and tension of warring emotions.[36]

Ashley Dukes offered Yeats the use of the Mercury Theatre in 1934. Like the Peacock Theatre, it had a small auditorium of

136 seats, though its stage was separated from the stalls (see Plate 32). Yeats's first plan was to produce *A Full Moon in March* with Ninette de Valois dancing as the Queen.[37] He set up a committee of actors, writers, designers, and dancers: Ashley Dukes, Edmund Dulac, T. S. Eliot, Margot Ruddock, Diaghilev's former *premier danseur* Rupert Doone, and Sir Frederick Ashton of the Camargo Society.[38] A season of poetic drama was arranged for 1935, including plays by Yeats, T. S. Eliot and W. H. Auden. Yeats suggested productions of *The Resurrection*, *The Player Queen*, and either *A Full Moon in March*, with Rupert Doone as the male dancer,[39] or, since he could 'permit little modification of the stage directions,' *Fighting the Waves*.[40] Unfortunately those arrangements did not work out. According to T. S. Eliot's producer, E. Martin Browne, 'Yeats was inaccessible and difficult; there was not sufficient assurance of support...; and Doone became involved in the Group's session at the Westminster.'[41] Ashley Dukes was able to bring *Murder in the Cathedral* from Canterbury to the Mercury in October 1935. Dukes has recalled Yeats's view that 'the success of the Abbey had been due to its deliberate limitation of appeal. 'Make your theatre difficult to find, difficult to know about,' he said to me. But he was glad when a poet's theatre in London drew large audiences, and he stood up crying 'Magnificent! Magnificent! at Eliot's *Murder in the Cathedral*.'[42]

During the production of *Murder in the Cathedral* Yeats attended a festival at the Little Theatre in honour of his seventieth birthday. Nancy Price, a member of the People's National Theatre Company, produced *The Pot of Broth*, *The Hour-Glass*, and *The Player Queen*.[43] Seeing his plays in performance gave Yeats the inspiration for a new play, *The Herne's Egg*, based on *The Player Queen*. He selected aspects of the play, omitting much of the political and sexual intrigues, and emphasizing instead the moment of confrontation. As in the last plays of Shakespeare and Ibsen, which 'present not a conflict but a vision of good and evil,'[44] the dances in *The Herne's Egg* present opposite modes of thought and action — Attracta and Congal, saint and swordsman.[45] The dramatic conflict of the earlier play is replaced by this complementary relationship. After the London production of *The Player*

Players and Painted Stage

Queen, Yeats wrote, 'I want to plunge myself into impersonal poetry, to get rid of the bitterness, irritation and hatred my work in Ireland has brought into my soul. I want to make a last song, sweet and exultant, a sort of European geets, or rather my *geeta*, not doctrine but song.'[46]

The story of Yeats's fifty years in the theatre is one of continual refinement of dramatic language and form. The combination of masks, dance, music, and expressive stage settings offered a highly flexible form for what Katharine Worth has called the 'complex modern states of self-consciousness'; after *Purgatory* and *The Death of Cuchulain*, 'the theatre was able to catch up with the modern movement in the arts.'[47] Worth's recent book, *The Irish Drama of Europe from Yeats to Beckett*, explores the development from Yeats's drama through the work of Beckett, O'Casey, T.S. Eliot, and Harold Pinter to the contemporary London theatre. Richard Taylor has drawn attention to the influence of Yeats's method of composition and stage presentation on the Theatre of the Absurd, and he interprets *The Herne's Egg*, with its 'mood of gaiety and abandon,' as a parody of the ideal world and an important stage in the development of an 'antiheroic theatre.'[48] Through a drama of masks and role playing Yeats uncovered a comic spirit seen most vividly in *The Green Helmet, The Player Queen, The Cat and the Moon*, and *The Herne's Egg*. He saw in tragedy too the portrayal of a great vitality of spirit. Tragedy is, in Yeats's words, 'a joy to the man who dies,' and 'the arts are all the bridal chambers of joy.'[49] T.R. Henn has pointed out that Yeats's plays lack the magnitude and momentum of Shakespeare's drama.[50] Yeats was concerned rather to isolate a character in the moment of 'existential confrontation': Deirdre's choice to die with Naoise, Cuchulain's raising the spear for endless battle, Emer's cry of renunciation, the Irish Republican Soldier's refusal of forgiveness, Decima's disastrous triumph as the Player Queen. In these extreme moments of crisis, the 'magnitude and momentum' found in Shakespeare has been replaced by an intensely vivid inner world that seeks its own magnitude in the imaginative response of the spectator. Drawing upon the full resources of drama in

The New Dance Drama

performance, the plays are a portrayal of what Yeats called the heroic act, 'an act done because a man is himself, because, being himself, he can ask of other men but room among remembered tragedies; a sacrifice of himself to himself almost.... So lonely is that ancient act, so great the pathos of its joy.'[51] At the Abbey production of *On Baile's Strand* in 1938, he saw Cuchulain as 'a heroic figure because he was creative joy separated from fear.'[52] Yeats's last play, *The Death of Cuchulain*, is an expression of that joy. The nearest in form to the Japanese Noh, it is a vivid portrayal of the complementary figures from his earlier work: Cuchulain and Fand, the Stroller and the Queen, the swordsman and the saint, Michael Gillane and Cathleen ni Houlihan, the martyred revolutionaries and Ireland. The mood of *The Death of Cuchulain* is exuberant, from the impassioned bitterness of Yeats's comic self-portrait as the Old Man in the Prologue, to the absorption of the dancing Emer, the nonchalance of Cuchulain in his last 'gay struggle without hope,' and the lively song of the Street Singer. We assent to reflection, Yeats thought, but we believe only in the myth, we love only the concrete. In contrast with the contemporary English theatre and its theme that 'bulks largely in the news,' Yeats placed the Irish:

We on the other hand are certain that nothing can give dignity to human nature but the character and energy of its expression. We do not even ask that it shall have dignity so long as it can burn away all that is not itself.[53]

Notes

CHAPTER 1

All quotations from the plays are from *The Collected Plays of W. B. Yeats* (London, 1960). The page numbers are given in parenthesis.

1. For contemporary uses of 'naturalism' and 'realism,' see R. N. Stromberg, ed., *Realism, Naturalism and Symbolism: Modes of Thought and Expression in Europe, 1848-1914* (London, 1968).
2. See Augusta Lady Gregory, *Our Irish Theatre* (London, 1913); Una Ellis Fermor, *The Irish Dramatic Movement* (London, 1939); James W. Flannery, *W. B. Yeats and the Idea of a Theatre: The Early Abbey Theatre in Theory and Practice* (Toronto, 1976).
3. *Explorations*, ed. Mrs. W. B. Yeats (London, 1962), 143.
3. Ibid., 143-144.
5. Ibid., 117.
6. *Autobiographies* (London, 1961), 416.
7. Ibid., 279.
8. Ibid., 283.
9. Ibid., 434.
10. *Essays and Introductions*, ed. Mrs. W. B. Yeats (London, 1961), 275.
11. Ann Saddlemyer, '"The Noble and the Beggar-Man': Yeats and Literary Nationalism,' in Robin Skelton and Ann Saddlemyer, eds., *The World of W. B. Yeats: Essays in Perspective* (Dublin, 1965), 26. See also Daniel Corkery, *Synge and Anglo-Irish Literature* (London, 1931).
12. *Explorations*, 156. For Yeats's indebtedness to Shelley's *Defence of Poetry*, with its emphasis on the practical benefits of the poetic vision in the development of nationality, see George Bornstein, *Yeats and Shelley* (Chicago and London, 1970), 60-66.
13. *Explorations*, 148. Yeats was greatly impressed by the London performance in 1908 of Pirandello's plays by Signor Grasso's Sicilian players. In an unpublished lecture, he contrasts a production of Galsworthy's *Justice* with the Sicilian players who 'have the old theme — the exposition of human life in human forms, for the sake of human life.' Quoted in William Becker, 'Yeats as a Playwright,' Ph.D. theses, Oxford University, 72.
14. *Explorations*, 242, 117.

Notes to pages 4-11

15. In *Samhain: 1904*, Yeats announced his plan to follow 'A.E.' and Synge in writing a play 'on the subject of *Deirdre*, with choruses somewhat in the Greek manner.' *Explorations*, 138.
16. Included in Liam Miller, 'W. B. Yeats and Stage Design at the Abbey Theatre,' with Yeats's comment from 'Literature and the Living Voice' (1906) that scenery should be 'little more than a suggestion — a pattern with recurring boughs and leaves of gold for a wood, a great green curtain with a red stencil upon it to carry the eye upward for a palace.' *Malahat Review* 16 (1970), 56-57.
17. *The Collected Plays of W. B. Yeats* (London, 1960), 171.
18. 'The Philosophy of Shelley's Poetry,' *Essays and Introductions*, 86. See also Yeats's comment that 'Our daily thought was certainly but the line of foam at the shallow edge of a vast luminous sea' in *Mythologies*, ed. Mrs. W. B. Yeats (London, 1959), 346. The action of several plays is set by the sea: *On Baile's Strand, The Green Helmet, The Golden Helmet, At the Hawk's Well, The Only Jealousy of Emer. The Shadowy Waters* is set in the midst of the sea. For Yeats's interest in the Neoplatonic tradition of Shelley's images — the tower, cave and river — see Bornstein, *Yeats and Shelley*, 77-94. See also Barton R. Friedman, *Adventures in the Deeps of the Mind: The Cuchulain Cycle of W. B. Yeats* (Princeton, 1977), 101.
19. The chess game occurs both in the Lugaidh and Edain legends. The literal and figurative meanings of this stage setting were first explored in David R. Clark, *W. B. Yeats and the Theatre of Desolate Reality* (Dublin, 1965), 32-41. See also Barton Friedman's discussion of this setting as 'a medium of symbolic communication' in *Adventures in the Deeps of the Mind*, 63-64.
20. In Yeats's poem 'Baile and Aillinn,' the god of love grants an escape to Edain and her lover, 'two swans...linked by a gold chain.' *The Collected Poems* (London, 1967), 459.
21. See also Barton Friedman's discussion of the 'identity of myth and truth' in *Deirdre. Adventures in the Deeps of the Mind*, 46.
22. *Autobiographies*, 494, 493.
23. Ibid., 493, 494.
24. Ibid., 195, 207.
25. Ibid., 469, 503. Barton Friedman interprets *Deirdre* as a play reflecting the conflict between 'desire for life and the demands of myth.' *Adventures in the Deeps of the Mind*, 63.
26. Denis de Rougement discusses the religious tradition behind the imagery of ecstasy and death in *L'amour et l'Occident* (Paris, 1936). Barton Friedman gives an account of the Musicians' lyric in relation to Nietzsche's tragic philosophy in *Adventures in the Deeps of the Mind*, 60-61.
27. Quoted in Lennox Robinson, 'The Man and the Dramatist,' *Scattering Branches*, ed. Stephen Gwynn (London, 1940), 96.
28. *The Image* (Dublin, 1910), 99-100.
29. Ibid., 101.
30. The Fay brothers, who trained the early Abbey actors, were influenced

Notes to page 12

in part by the naturalistic acting style of Andre Antoine's company at his celebrated avant garde theatre in Paris, Théâtre Libre. See Gabrielle Fallon, *The Abbey and the Actor* (Dublin, 1969), 14-30. Frank O'Connor, on the other hand, thinks the Fay brothers' style was closer to Yeats's ideal: 'It is undoubtedly the style of acting that was common in European universities up to Shakespeare's day and associated with the production of Seneca's plays. It is an almost purely literary style, and one can summarize it by saying that no one speaks when moving and no one moves when someone else is speaking, so that the attention is not distracted from the spoken word.' *The Backward Look: A Survey of Irish Literature* (London, 1967), 169.
31 Cited in Ann Saddlemyer, '"Worn Out With Dreams": Dublin's Abbey Theatre,' Skelton and Saddlemyer, *The World of W. B. Yeats*, 118.
32 *Autobiographies*, 483.

CHAPTER 2

1. *The Letters of W. B. Yeats*, ed. Allan Wade (New York, 1955), 567.
2. Gordon Craig, *Index to the Story of My Days: Some Memoirs of Edward Gordon Craig, 1872-1907* (London, 1957), 239. See Yeats's letter to the *Saturday Review* in Wade, *Letters*, 365-366.
3. 'I have seen all the costumes too, and hope to get patterns. He costumed the whole play — 30 or 40 people I should say — for £25.' Wade, *Letters*, 380.
4. *Explorations*, ed. Mrs. W. B. Yeats (London, 1962), 178. The Victorian theatre was the culmination of the type of theatre developed in the late fifteenth century in Italy by architects such as Palladio and Serlio who used the new technique of painted perspectives.
5. 'Letter' to the *Evening Telegraph*, 9 January 1911, quoted in Denis Bablet, *Edward Gordon Craig* (Paris, 1962), trans. Daphne Woodward (London, 1966), 130.
6. *Essays and Introductions*, ed. Mrs. W. B. Yeats (London, 1961), 366.
7. Ibid., 375.
8. *Explorations*, 4.
9. *Essays and Introductions*, 100.
10. *Explorations*, 74.
11. *Essays and Introductions*, 364.
12. Ibid., 383.
13. Ibid., 370.
14. *Explorations*, 163.
15. Wade, *Letters*, 371. Ann Saddlemyer notes Yeats's great but underestimated debt to Craig, though she judges Yeats's drama as an essentially private rather than public art, '"The Heroic Discipline of the Looking-Glass': W. B. Yeats's search for Dramatic Design,' in Robin Skelton and Ann Saddlemyer, eds., *The World of W. B. Yeats: Essays in Perspective* (Dublin, 1965), 96-99, 103. Barton Friedman remarks that 'Craig, apparently by independent courses, had arrived at a theory of drama close to Yeats's.' *Adventures in the Deeps of the Mind: The Cuchulain Cycle of W. B. Yeats* (Princeton, 1977), 16.
16. Yeats wrote to Lady Gregory, 'I am also bringing my model theatre and have a plan of giving two lectures in the autumn. One on a simpler theatre, and one on the speaking of verse to notes.' Wade, *Letters*, 375. William Fay has described Yeats's demonstrations with Craig's model theatre: 'It was a simple horizon cloth with some rocks and trees in the foreground, painted in monochrome, but lit in three different colours. For the first time it produced a feeling of atmosphere in stage lighting.' 'The Poet and the Actor,' *Scattering Branches*, ed. Stephen Gwynn (London, 1940), 133. Fay's description suggests that the model was the set for *Dido and Aeneas*, which Yeats saw in 1900 and 1901. The use of a model theatre to illustrate lectures was standard practice; Craig first saw the combination of electric lights, gauze, sidelighting, music, and dance at the theatre in Bushey, when the Bavarian artist Hubert von Herkomer used a model set in 1892 to illustrate his talks. Edward Craig, *Gordon Craig: The Story of His Life* (London, 1968), 78-79.

17 Wade, *Letters*, 380.
18 In this letter to John Quinn, Yeats wrote that Craig 'is the great innovator here in the matter of scenery and has begun experiments which may perhaps revolutionize the whole art.' From the files of The Macmillan Company (New York), *Variorum Plays*, 1167. *Where There is Nothing* was produced by Granville Barker at the Royal Court Theatre on June 26, 27, and 28, 1904, with Edith Craig as one of the tinkers. Wade, *Letters*, 382-383.
19 Wade, *Letters*, 375.
20 Ibid., 394.
21 Janet Leeper comments on Craig's production of *The Vikings:* 'Colour was used in combination with the movement of the stage, and we already see here — in 1900-3 — the beginning of what was to lead to Diaghilev's Russian Ballet.' In 1906-1907, Craig planned a ballet, *Psyche*, which Diaghilev refused because he thought it too daring. *Edward Gordon Craig: Designs for the Theatre* (London, 1948), 8, 18.
22 *Essays and Introductions*, 100-101.
23 Wade, *Letters*, 398. Yeats may have exaggerated the distraction; Wade notes that the musical director Martin Shaw 'did not use the words supplied by Yeats but returned to William Archer's version of the song as being more like Ibsen; small wonder that Yeats could not distinguish his words during the performance.'
24 Wade, *Letters*, 456.
25 *Variorum Plays*, 1293; *Explorations*, 108.
26 *Explorations*, 110. For Yeats's versions of Sophocles' Oedipus plays, see chapter 4, this book.
27 An unsigned reveiw of Craig's, in his theatre journal *The Mask* 4 (1911-1912): 343. *Plays for an Irish Theatre* (London and Stratford-upon-Avon, 1911), includes four of Craig's drawings.
28 In December 1911, Craig's screens appeared for the second time, in Stanislavski's production of *Hamlet* at the Moscow Art Theatre.
29 Craig's note on the endpaper of his copy of Serlio. Edward Craig, *Gordon Craig*, 235.
30 This series of wood engravings was published in *Scene* (1923).
31 Craig thought the Abbey Theatre never understood the principle behind his screens; 'hovering, hiding, advancing, retreating,' they were to create an impression of timelessness and motion. Craig's letter to Ann Saddlemyer, 27 February, 1960, quoted in *The World of W. B. Yeats*, 96. Craig was disappointed that Stanislavski chose to keep the screens stationary during the 1911 production of *Hamlet* because several members of the cast and stage crew had been injured by a screen falling over during rehearsal. E. Craig, *Gordon Craig*, 258. Craig's scenery was not often used in these early years because of difficulties he created himself. He took out a patent for the screens and insisted on supervising all productions.
32 Wade, *Letters*, 546.
33 Ibid.
34 Ibid.

Notes to pages 18-20

35 For discussions of Yeats's work with Craig, see also James W. Flannery, *W. B. Yeats and the Idea of a Theatre: The Early Abbey Theatre in Theory and Practice* (Toronto, 1976), 245-78; and Liam Miller, *The Noble Drama of W. B. Yeats* (Dublin, 1977), 147-181, which includes reproductions of Yeats's notebook of sketches for stage settings using Craig's screens.

36 Wade, *Letters*, 555. The Abbey architect Joseph Holloway took quite a different view of the new scenery. After a visit in November 1910, he wrote, 'I called in at the Abbey and saw the stagehands setting Gordon Craig's new idea of scenery — a series of square box-like pillars, saffron hued, with saffron background, wings, sky pieces and everything. The entire setting struck me as like peas, only on a big scale, of the blocks I as a child built houses of. As Yeats never played with blocks in his youth, Gordon Craig's childish ideas give him keen pleasure now.' Quoted in Liam Miller, 'W. B. Yeats and Stage Design at the Abbey Theatre,' Malahat Review 16 (1970), 59-60. The screens were still at the Abbey in the late forties. See Eric Bentley, *In Search of Theatre* (London, 1954), 228.

37 The plays were revived in 1911 (*The Hour-Glass* in January, *The Land of Heart's Desire* in February, *The Countess Cathleen* in December). After revision and production during the winter, each was restaged in 1912 versions (*The Land of Heart's Desire* in February 1912, *The Countess Cathleen* in September, *The Hour-Glass* in November).

38 Yeats wrote in June 1912, 'During the last year I have spent much time altering 'The Countess Cathleen' and 'The Land of Heart's Desire' that they might be a part of the repertory of the Abbey Theatre. I had written them before I had any practical experience.' *Variorum Plays*, 1291.

39 Wade, *Letters*, 567-568.

40 Richard Ellmann, *Yeats: The Man and the Masks* (London, 1949), 131.

41 The play was officially entitled *The Hour Glass: A Morality*.

42 In 1904 Yeats complained that this play shared with the early lyrics 'an exaggeration of sentiment and sentimental beauty.' Wade, *Letters*, 434.

43 Yeats used this type of stage space in earlier Abbey productions of *The Golden Helmet* (1908) and *The Green Helmet* (1910). According to William Fay, Craig's new method of lighting and staging was first tried at the Abbey for its opening play, *On Baile's Strand*, set in a room with a view beyond. 'The Poet and the Actor,' *Scattering Branches*, ed. Stephen Gwynn (London, 1940), 133-134. Barton Friedman describes the possibilities offered by the platform stage in his discussion of *On Baile's Strand, Adventures in the Deeps of the Mind*, 34.

44 *Variorum Plays*, 192.

45 The *tableaux vivants* were staged in January 1899, as part of the promotion of the play. Wade, *Letters*, 306n.

46 Wade, *Letters*, 308. Yeats's letter is part of the debate in the *Daily Chronicle*, January 1899, between William Archer, who suggested that the play be staged in an expensive, elaborate set, and George Moore, who hoped it would be staged with neither scenery nor costumes.

47 *Variorum Plays*, 1291.

48 See M. J. Sidnell, 'Yeats's First Work for the Stage: The Earliest Versions of "The Countess Cathleen,"' in D. E. S. Maxwell and S. B. Bushrui, eds., *W. B. Yeats: Centenary Essays on the Art of W. B. Yeats* (Ibadan, 1965), 182-183. Yeats found the story for this play in a collection of Irish folklore and considered it the Irish equivalent of the Greek parable of Alcestis. *Variorum Plays*, 170.
49 *Variorum Plays*, 53.
50 *Explorations*, 163.
51 *Variorum Plays*, 1291.
52 Peter Ure, *Yeats the Playwright* (London, 1963), 29.
53 'The Plays,' in Denis Donoghue and J. R. Mulryne, eds., *An Honoured Guest* (New York, 1966), 153. Frank O'Connor thought Yeats an 'absolute master' on the one-act miracle play form, though he could not advise on longer constructions done at the Abbey Theatre, for instance, Synge's *Playboy of the Western World*, which, according to O'Connor, makes the mistake of not revealing before Christy's bragging scene that his father was not really dead. *The Backward Look: A Survey of Irish Literature* (London, 1967), 170.
54 Lady Wilde's story, from her *Ancient Legend of Ireland* (1887), is reprinted in *Variorum Plays*, 640-644. The original prose version of Yeats's play, produced at the Abbey in 1903, was reprinted with minor revisions until 1911. The final prose version of 1922 includes the new ending developed in the verse versions. After producing the 1911 prose version in Craig's scenery, Yeats wrote the first verse for a production the following year (November 1912). This version, printed in 1913 in Craig's theatre journal, *The Mask*, was followed by another verse version with a new ending (1914). The final verse version (1922) includes the 'medieval Latin' passages. See S. B. Bushrui, '"The Hour-Glass": Yeats's Revisions, 1903-1922,' Maxwell and Bushrui, *Centenary Essays*, 189-216.
55 T. R. Henn calls these changes in language the 'strata on a cliff face.' *The Lonely Tower* (London, 1965), 281. I use Dr. Henn's two examples of verse.
56 *Variorum Plays*, 592, 594.
57 Henn, *Lonely Tower*, 281.
58 *Essays and Introductions*, 277, 279.
59 From Yeats's interview in 'Hearth and Home' (November 1912), quoted by Craig in *The Mask* 7 (1914): 141.
60 Ursula Bridge, ed., *W. B. Yeats and T. Sturge Moore: Their Correspondence 1901-1937* (London, 1953), 5.
61 Ibid., 5
62 From the Ellis-Yeats edition of Blake, quoted in Edward Engelberg, *The Vast Design* (Toronto, 1964), 3. See also Craig's comment that 'the movement of two and four which is the square, the movement of one and three which is the circle. There is ever that which is masculine in the square and ever that which is feminine in the circle.' *On the Art of the Theatre* (London, 1957), 52.
63 Wade, *Letters*, 554.

64. 'The Artists of the Theatre of the Future' (1907) reprinted in Craig, *On the Art of the Theatre*, 13. See also Craig's comparison of acting styles: 'I should say that the face of Irving was the connecting link between that spasmodic and ridiculous expression of the human face as used by the theatres of the last few centuries, and the masks which will be used in place of the human face in the near future.' 12-13.
65. Quoted in Leeper, *Edward Gordon Craig*, 46.
66. Wade, *Letters*, 554.
67. Yeats's to Craig, 3 November 1911, quoted in the exhibition catalogue 'Gordon Craig et la Renouvellement du Theatre,' (Paris, 1962), 61.
68. Wade, *Letters*, 425.
69. *Variorum Plays*, 646, 577.
70. In 'Discoveries,' Yeats called argument 'almost the only kind of passion that displays itself in our daily life.' *Essays and Introductions*, 275. Lady Wilde wrote of the Wise Man that 'one of his great triumphs was in argument.' The Fool is Yeats's own addition to the original story.
71. Ibid., 292.
72. Yeats added the Latin passages to remove some repetitions in the verse. *Variorum Plays*, 646. These additions are usually dismissed as unnecessary and undramatic.
73. *Essays and Introductions*, 266.
74. Bushrui, 'The Hour-Glass,' 203-204.
75. See Richard Ellmann: 'Yeats gives Babylon the role of ushering in Christianity because the astronomers there, who plotted the stars, helped to reduce man's status in relation to the universe by promulgating the inhuman abstractions of science.' *The Identity of Yeats* (New York, 1954), 262.
76. See also Yeats's essay 'The Queen and the Fool' (1901) in *The Celtic Twilight* (London, 1902), 194.
77. Wade, *Letters*, 378. G.C. Duggan cites Bourgeois's 'John Millington Synge and the Irish Theatre' (1913) in his definition of the stage Irishman, called Pat, Paddy, or Teague, with fiery red hair and a gift for blarney. *The Stage Irishman* (London, 1937), 288-289.
78. See also Seanchan's remark in *The King's Threshold*:

> But why were you born crooked?
> What bad poet did your mothers listen to
> That you were born so crooked?   (133)

79. At this time, Yeats was preparing a version of *Oedipus Rex* for the Abbey. (See chapter 5, 74-76, this book). See also Mircea Eliade on the traditional metaphors of sight and blindness in *Myth and Reality*, trans. Willard R, Trask (New York, 1963), 114-138.
80. In 1930, Yeats recalled that a French etching of an old wingless, elongated angel armed like a knight had been his source for the angels in the early final scene of *The Countess Cathleen*. *Explorations*, 305-306. Yeats wrote that 'Craig evidently wants to keep what is superhuman from being inhuman.' Wade, *Letters*, 554.
81. *Variorum Plays*, 601.

Notes to pages 30-33

82 Una Ellis-Fermor, *The Irish Dramatic Movement* (London, 1939), 108-109. Miss Ellis-Fermor suggests that the play's kinship lies not with allegorical moralities of the middle ages but with the modern symbolic morality plays, such as the final act of *Peer Gynt* and parts of *Everyman*.
83 *Variorum Plays*, 584.
84 The Fool's money bag is similar to the Amadan's 'shining vessel of some enchantment or wisdom or dream too powerful for mortal brains.' 'The Queen and the Fool,' 192.
85 This episode is a revision of the episode Yeats disliked: 'When the Wise Man abused himself before the Fool I was always ashamed.... Nor I have made my philosopher accept God's will, whatever it is, and find his courage again.' *Variorum Plays*, 645-646.
86 'The Queen and the Fool,' 193.
87 'The Actor and the Über-Marionette,' (1907), reprinted in Craig, *On the Art of the Theatre*, 74. (See chapter 3, 48-49, this book.)
88 'The Queen and the Fool,' 192.
89 See also Yeats's poem, 'Another Song of a Fool':

> This great purple butterfly,
> Is the prism of my hands,
> Has a learning in his eye
> Not a poor fool understands.
>
> Once he lived a schoolmaster
> With a stark, denying look;
> A string of scholars went in fear
> Of his great birch and his great book.
>
> Like the clangour of a bell,
> Sweet and harsh, harsh and sweet,
> That is how he learnt so well
> To take the roses for his meat.
>
> *The Collected Poems*, 191-192

90 *Essays and Introductions*, 271.
91 'Is Poetic Drama Born Again?', *The Mask* 5 (1912-1913): 291. (The volume includes two articles by Jack B. Yeats on producing his plays for children using a miniature stage similar to Craig's.) In 1913 Yeats seriously considered joining Craig in Florence as literary advisor for 'a big scheme of poetic drama.' Wade, *Letters*, 577. The year before, 'The Society of the Theatre' was formed, including Yeats, Craig, Augustus John, William Poel, J. Martin Harvey, Constantin Stanislavski, Tomasso Salvini, Cecil Sharp, and Ezra Pound. A prospectus, probably written by Craig, announced that the Society

> aims at creating a dramatic movement which shall appeal to the theatrical rather than to the literary aspect of drama. By 'theatrical' is meant that form of stage production which makes an appeal to the senses through the imagination rather than to the intellect.
>
> The Society has adopted the idea of Gordon Craig, and is formed

Notes to page 33

to promote discussion of the idea, and to try to establish a School for the Art of the Theatre, with Gordon Craig as authoritative director.
Allardyce Nicoll, *English Drama: 1900-1930* (Cambridge, 1973), 103-104.

92 *Towards a New Theatre*, 68. Yeats urged his publisher to publish an edition of his theatre criticism with drawings by Craig and Robert Gregory: 'Coming at this moment when people have in their memories the Reinhardt productions, the scenery and costumes of the Russian ballet, the Barker productions of Shakespeare — all examples of the new decorative method — it would probably get considerable attention. It would contain the only serious criticism of the new craft of the Theatre. It is the exact moment for it.' Wade, *Letters*, 579. Such a volume did not appear until *Plays and Controversies* (1923), and then only the dance plays were illustrated.

93 Yeats to Craig, 29 July 1913, in the Gordon Craig Collection, Bibliothèque de l'Arsenal, Paris, quoted in Bablet, *Edward Gordon Craig*, 130. In 1913, Yeats arranged the Dublin exhibition of Craig's theatre designs, including the model for the 1911 production of *Hamlet* in Moscow. Miller, 'W. B. Yeats and Stage Design at the Abbey,' 60.

Notes to pages 34-35

CHAPTER 3

1 Padraic Colum, 'Poet's Progress: W. B. Yeats in the Theatre [a review of *The Collected Plays*],' *Theatre Arts Monthly* (December 1935), 941-942. The new style of dramatic speech was based on Yeats's close work with the Abbey players and appears also in the volume of poetry entitled *The Green Helmet* (1910).
2 *The Irish Times* (September 9, 1911), 8.
3 Productions included *Interlude of Youth, Second Shepherd's Play, Nativity Play, The Annunciation, Flight to Egypt,* and *The World and the Chylde.* Augusta Lady Gregory, *Our Irish Theatre* (London, 1913), 264-265. In 1914 Monck set up the Maddermarket Theatre in Norwich for productions of medieval plays. He left Dublin after only two seasons, due partly to Lady Gregory's insistence that the Abbey present Irish work. Monck, despite Yeats's comment to the Abbey audience, was English.
4 Yeats wanted an apron stage for the original Abbey Theatre, as he explained in 1904: 'The necessities of a builder have torn from us, all unwill as we were, the apron, as the portion of the platform that came in front of the proscenium used to be called, and we must submit to the picture-making of the modern stage. We would have preferred to be able to return occasionally to the old stage for statue-making, of gestures.' *Explorations*, ed. Mrs. W. B. Yeats (London, 1962), 173. In one of the experimental productions, Yeats worked the lights from the balcony. As he explained in a note to the new version of *The Countess Cathleen*, 'The new end is particularly suited to the Abbey stage, where the stage platform can be brought out in front of the proscenium and have a flight of steps at one side up which the Angel comes, crossing towards the back of the stage at the opposite side. The principal lighting is from two arc lights in the balcony which throw their lights into the faces of the players, making footlights unnecessary.' *Variorum Plays*, 173-174. The reconstruction of the Abbey stage is mentioned in *Joseph Holloway's Abbey Theatre. A Selection from his Unpublished Journal, Impressions of a Dublin Playgoer*, 140. See also James W. Flannery, *W. B. Yeats and the Idea of a Theatre: The Early Abbey Theatre in Theory and Practice* (Toronto, 1976), 272-275.
5 Noh drama, the theatre of the Japanese court from the fifteenth to the seventeenth century, was developed from older dance forms by Kwanami and his son Zeami in the early fifteenth century and passed on through specially trained families. Ernest Fenollosa, an American scholar and diplomat, played an important role, in perservering the Japanese traditional heritage. After his death in London in 1908, his widow asked Ezra Pound to edit his manuscript of Noh plays in 1913. For a detailed discussion of Yeats's assimilation of Noh technique from the Fenollosa manuscript, see Richard Taylor, *The Drama of W. B. Yeats: Irish Myth and the Japanese No* (New Haven and London, 1976).

Notes to pages 35-37

6   Yeats had seen the drawings in the British Museum collection, and similar illustrations in most issues of *The Mask*, from 1908 onward. At that time, only a few Noh plays had been translated. D.J. Gordon, in *W. B. Yeats: Images of a Poet* (Manchester, 1961), mentions these books: 1892, Sir Edwin Arnold's translation of a Noh play and a poem describing the Noh dance; in 1901, Osman Edwards's *Japanese Plays and Playfellows* with an illustrated chapter on the religious drama; 1901, Japanese actors in London; 1906, M.A. Hink's 'The Art of Dancing in Japan' in *Fortnightly Review*; 1910, Marie Stopes's description of the Noh in *A Journal from Japan*; 1912, Marie Stopes's *Plays of Old Japan*; 1916, Oswald Sickert's letters from Japan to Charles Ricketts, published in 1921 in Arthur Waley's book, *The Nō Plays of Japan*.

7   *Essays and Introductions*, ed. Mrs. W. B. Yeats (London, 1961), 240. Early students of Yeats's dance plays praised Ezra Pound and the Noh drama for transforming Yeats's poetic and dramatic work, but with increased knowledge of the Noh conventions and renewed interest in Yeats's early work, scholars such as F.A.C. Wilson, Thomas Parkinson and Richard Ellmann have noted the similarities between Yeats's early and later work, after he met Pound. K.L. Goodwin draws the same conclusion in his discussions of the revisions of Yeats's poems in *The Influence of Ezra Pound* (London, 1966).

8   *Variorum Plays*, 315. See also Graham Martin's discussion of the order of Yeats's poems in 'The Wild Swans at Coole,' in *An Honoured Guest*, ed. Denis Donoghue and J.R. Mulryne (New York, 1966), 54-72. As Thomas Parkinson remarks, Yeats 'makes a statement when he acts as editor, maker of books. He shapes a poetic construct even when he is editing, say, *The Oxford Book of Modern Verse*, and the statement made by Yeats in selecting for that anthology was a definition of a poetics.' *W. B. Yeats, The Later Poetry* (University of California Press, Berkeley, 1964), 55.

9   *Variorum Plays*, 1293.

10 Ernest Fenollosa and Ezra Pound, *'Noh' or Accomplishment, A Study of the Classical Stage in Japan* (London, 1916), 17.

11 *The Letters of W. B. Yeats*, ed. Allan Wade (New York, 1955), 587. Gordon Bottomley has described the Japanese element in Ricketts' stage designs: 'shortly after [the 1909 London] production of *King Lear* [Ricketts] was asked to design this play again for the Japanese for which he afterward did his later *Salome*.... He flung himself delightedly into this task, as though he had never touched the play before; and, taking the motives of his previous mounting, he executed a marvelous fantasy on them, heightening them with touches and poses and patterns that brought the drawings into relation with the prints of Utamaro and Kiyonage — expressing them in terms that gave them Japanese appeal, without destroying the reference to Shakespeare.' 'Charles Ricketts R.A.,' *Arts Theatre Monthly*, May 1932), 382, 391.

12 Wade, *Letters*, 595.

13 *Essays and Introductions*, 233.

Notes to pages 38-41

14 For Yeats's interest in Shelley's Neoplatonic images of the journey, see George Bornstein, *Yeats and Shelley* (Chicago and London, 1970), 77-94, and Barton Friedman, *Adventures in the Deeps of the Mind*: 101.
15 There are varying interpretations of Cuchulain's exit. Helen Vendler sees Cuchulain as 'the hero who can tell the true immortality of brief remembered glory from false longevity,' but F. A. C. Wilson sees Cuchulain's final action as failure. Harold Bloom thinks that Cuchulain, far from asserting what Mrs. Vendler calls 'moral heroism,' lacks the self-consciousness of a tragic hero. Peter Ure remarks that Cuchulain's courage transforms him into a victim, and the play enacts the 'contradictory nature of heroic courage.' Helen Vendler, *Yeats's Vision and the Later Plays* (Cambridge, Mass., 1963), 213; F. A. C. Wilson, *Yeats's Iconography* (London, 1960), 67; Harold Bloom, *Yeats* (New York and Oxford, 1970), 296-297; Peter Ure, *Yeats the Playwright* (London, 1963), 72.
16 For Yeats's adaptation of Shakespeare in this play, see Rupin Desai, *Yeats's Shakespeare* (Evanston, Ill., 1971), 160-166. See also Friedman, *Adventures in the Deeps of the Mind*, 34.
17 Friedman, *Adventures in the Deeps of the Mind*, 42. Friedman also remarks on the distancing effect of the final scene: 'To have the Fool Narrate Cuchulain's ordeal is to turn Cuchulain himself, as he had earlier been turned by the Fool's song, into an image in the Fool's mind, to turn the fight into a tale the Fool tells.' (40). See also Friedman's remarks on Yeats's adaptation of the final scene of Robert Bridges' *The Return of Ulysses*, in which Ulysses slaying Penelope's suitors is narrated by her maid. 40-1.
18 Antonin Artaud gave similar reasons for his adaptation of the Balinese theatre: 'In a word, the Balinese have realized, with the utmost rigor, the idea of pure theatre, where everything, conception and realization alike, has value, has existence only in proportion to its degree of objectification *on the stage*.' *The Theater and its Double*, trans. Mary Caroline Richards (New York, 1958), 53.
19 *Essays and Introductions*, 230.
20 Raymond Williams says that in *Four Plays for Dancers*, 'The design of the plays is not only visual. In each case the song, which accompanies the folding and unfolding of the cloth which marks the beginning and end of the play, provides an image which is at the centre of the revelation into which the play then moves.' *Drama from Ibsen to Brecht* (London, 1968), 126.
21 See also Richard Taylor's discussion of the similar pair of characters in *Yōrō*, an unpublished Noh play that Yeats read in the Fenollosa manuscript, in 'Assimilation and Accomplishment: Nō Drama and an Unpublished Source for *At the Hawk's Well*,' Robert O'Driscoll and Lorna Reynolds, eds., *Yeats and the Theatre* (Toronto and London, 1975), 137-158.
22 *Essays and Introductions*, 235. 'Presentational' is commonly used for Oriental dance and drama, where the actor's performance is built from

Notes to pages 42-45

'artificial signs which have been conventionally established.' Elder Olson, *Tragedy and the Theory of Drama* (Detroit, 1961), 24. Raymond Williams describes the contrasting modern actor's performance as 'Behaviour': 'the kind of action, as in *The Seagull*, where the words and movement have no direct and necessary relation, but derive, as it were separately, from a conception of "probable behaviour" in the circumstances presented. Words and movements often equally communicate with dramatic experience, but not in a design of "acted speech"; the speech...is often separate from the "acting"'. *Drama in Performance* (London, 1972), 172.

23 *The Noh Drama: Ten Plays from the Japanese, Selected and Translated by the special Noh Committee* (Tokyo and Rutland, Vermont, 1955; Rutland, Vermont, 1969), xii.
24 Quoted in Arthur Waley, *The Nō Plays of Japan, with Letters by Oswald Sickert* (London, 1921), 310-311.
25 Yasuo Nakamura, *Noh: The Classical Theatre*, trans. Don Kenny (New York and Tokyo, 1971), 158-159.
26 Ibid., 54. Bertolt Brecht's 'alienation-effect' was derived from his interest in the 'presentational' aspects of Oriental theatre, especially from the Kabuki performances he saw in Moscow as a young man. His essay, 'Alienation Effects in Chinese Theatre,' first published in 1936, is reprinted in *Brecht on Theatre*, trans. and with notes by John Willett (New York, 1964), 91-99. In *'Noh' or Accomplishment* Pound included Fenollosa's comment that 'The discipline of the actor is a moral one. He is trained to revere his profession, to make it a sacred act thus to impersonate a hero. He yields himself up to possession by the character. He acts as if he knew himself to be a god, and after the performance he is generally quite exhausted.' 122.
27 *Variorum Plays*, 1305.
28 *Essays and Introductions*, 195. Yeats wrote in his edition of Blake, 'Sometimes the mystical student, bewildered by the different systems, forgets for a moment that the history of moods is the history of the universe, and asks where is the final statement — the complete doctrine. The universe is itself that doctrine and statement. All others are partial, for it alone is the symbol of the infinite thought which is in turn symbolic of the universal mood we name God.' Quoted in Richard Ellmann, *The Identity of Yeats* (New York, 1954), 59.
29 *Essays and Introductions*, 277.
30 *Mythologies*, ed. Mrs. W. B. Yeats (London, 1959), 335.
31 *Noh Drama*, 2: xxiii.
32 Fenollosa and Pound, *'Noh' or Accomplishment*, 194, 196-197. In an early draft of the play Yeats emphasized the antagonism in the spirit world. Bricriu and Fand battle for power through possession of Emer and Cuchulain. Helen Vendler remarks that 'Emer's love for Cuchulain has been used as a pawn in a strategy of the immortals, and our last glimpse of Fand and Bricriu shows them trying to outride each other to the court of their common sovereign, the sea god, Manannan, to have their quarrel judged.' Vendler, *Yeats's Vision and the Later*

Plays, 222. See also Taylor, *The Drama of W. B. Yeats*, 141-143.
33 *Mythologies*, 346. The original title for the play was 'A Sword Blade Against the Foam.' Vendler, *Yeats's Vision and the Later Plays*, 220.
34 Taylor, *The Drama of W. B. Yeats*, 145.
35 *Mythologies*, 341. The passage is part of Yeats's discussion of psychoanalytic dream theory and his view of its limitations: 'The doctors of medicine have discovered that certain dreams of the night, for I do not grant them all, are the day's unfulfilled desire, and that our terror of desires condemned by the conscience has distorted and disturbed our dreams. They have only studied the breaking into dream of elements that have remained unsatisfied without purifying discouragement. We can satisfy in life a few of our passions and each passion but a little.'
36 Helen Vendler takes issue with F. A. C. Wilson on his assignment of these lines to a dialogue between the women. She suggests that the first two lines are Emer's address to Fand, and the rest of the stanza, Fand's to Emer. She is inclined, on the basis of this last stanza, to see the whole song as a 'dialogue of two warring positions.' Vendler, *Yeats's Vision and the Later Plays*, 233. The structural similarity between Fand and Eithne Inguba, which I have pointed out, suggests that a dialogue between Emer and Fand is also one between Emer and Eithne Inguba.
37 *Essays and Introductions*, 226.
38 First published in *The Mask* and reprinted in *On the Art of the Theatre*. See also Craig's article, 'A Note on Marionnettes,' written under the pseudonym of Adolf Furst: 'Each little figure, strangely human in its response,... gazing before it with eyes as inscrutable as those which yet meet ours from under the quiet brows of the gods of Egypt and Etruria.... that impassive gaze, that air of seeing *beyond* all the transitory and the accidental, still proclaim for the marionette his kinship with the grave stone images of the ancient eastern world.' *The Mask* 2 (1909-1910): 76. Barton Friedman discusses Yeats's and Craig's interest in puppets in relation to Blake's view of the creative process, *Adventures in the Deeps of the Mind*, 16-17.
39 'The Actor and the Über-Marionnette,' reprinted in Craig, *On the Art of the Theatre*, London, 1957, 56, 58.
40 Ibid., 74-75.
41 *Essays and Introductions*, 224-225. In an essay on Max Reinhardt's small theatre in Berlin, the Kammerspiele, Heinz Herald remarked that 'while the framed stage has a tendency to analyze, the Arena makes the concrete part of life appear still more concrete.' *Max Reinhardt and his Theatre*, ed. Oliver M. Sayler (New York, 1924), 152. For a discussion of the problems of the proscenium stage, see the interview with Paul Baker, an American producer who designed the Ruth Taylor Theatre in San Antonio, Texas, and assisted Frank Lloyd Wright in the design of the Frank Lloyd Wright Theatre in Dallas, in 'Flexible Theatrical Space [an interview with Paul Baker by Richard Schechner],' *The Drama Review*, 12, no. 3 (Spring 1968): 93.
42 *Essays and Introductions*, 232.
43 *Variorum Plays*, 777.

Notes to pages 50-56

44 *Essays and Introductions*, 230-231.
45 *The Collected Plays of W. B. Yeats* (London, 1960), 208.
46 Ure, *Yeats the Playwright*, 115. My discussion of *Calvary* is indebted to Professor Ure's remarks.
47 Ibid., 119.
48 For Yeats's story of Chance and Choice and the throwing of the dice, see *Variorum Plays*, 790. See also Wilson, *Yeats's Iconography*, 202. G. R. S. Mead's 'The Sacred Dance of Jesus' is often cited as a source for Yeats's dance. Mead's last example of the sacred dance, which contrasts vividly with Yeats's dance in *Calvary*, is taken from a description in Saint Augustine's letters: Jesus bids the disciples, before his betrayal, to form a ring round him. 'Then follows the mystery-dance of this Passion, the earliest Passion-play of Christendom. The neo-phyte is overwhelmed with the seeming horror of it, the setting at naught apparently, of the sacred person of the Man of Sorrows; he loses courage, and is assured he cannot understand the real joy of it until he is finally perfected. "If thou hadst known how to suffer, thou wouldst have had power not to suffer. Be content to suffer, and thou shalt not have to suffer. That which thou knowest not, I myself will teach thee. I am thou God."' *The Quest*, 2, no. 1 (October 1910): 47, 64-66.
49 Katharine Worth, *The Irish Drama of Europe from Yeats to Beckett* (London, 1978), 179.
50 *Variorum Plays*, 790.
51 *Essays and Introductions*, 234.
52 David R. Clark, *W. B. Yeats and the Theatre of Desolate Reality* (Dublin, 1965), 57.
53 F. A. C. Wilson remarks on the similarity between Yeats's play and Lady Gregory's *Dervorgilla* (1911), which includes the same act of refusal: Dervorgilla learns that the young people prefer to hate her youthful betrayal of Ireland than to forgive her later repentance. *Yeats's Iconography*, 208-209.
54 Fenollosa and Pound, *'Noh' or Accomplishment*, 147-148.
55 Reiko Tsukimura says that Yeats 'uses the hawk's dance not only for the evocation of an emotion but for the development of his plot.' 'A Comparison of Yeats's *At the Hawk's Well* and its Noh version, *Taka No Izumi*,' *Literature East and West*, 11, no. 4 (December 1967): 397.
56 Carole H. Smith, *T. S. Eliot's Dramatic Theory and Practice* (New Haven and London, 1963), 62n.
57 These plays are discussed further in chapters 4 and 5, this book.
58 For a detailed study of the revisions of *The Player Queen*, and reproductions of the manuscripts, see Curtis Bradford, ed., *W. B. Yeats: The Writing of The Player Queen* (DeKalb, Ill., 1977).
59 *Variorum Plays*, 1301. For Yeats's sketches of stage settings for his and Lady Gregory's plays, using Craig's screens, see Flannery, *W. B. Yeats and the Idea of a Theatre*, Plate 21, and Liam Miller, *The Noble Drama of W. B. Yeats* (Dublin, 1977), Plates 40-45. See Plate 7, this book. After the Stage Society's London production in May 1919, in which Maire O'Neill played Decima and Edith Evans Nona, the Abbey produced the

Notes to pages 57-61

play in December 1919, with Gordon Craig's daughter May as Nona. Joseph Holloway wrote of the Abbey production that 'its unfolding is set in so picturesque an environment that it charmed the eye, if it didn't wholly satisfy the mind.' *Joseph Holloway's Abbey Theatre*, 206.

60 See also Yeats's comment in *Plays for an Irish Theatre* (1911) that he wanted 'an even or almost even surface whereon the players are outlines clearly that we may see their movements and feel their importance.' *Variorum Plays*, 1300.

61 *Variorum Plays*, 761. Eric Bentley disagreed with Yeats's claim, and he emphasized the Irish setting in his 1951 production at the Abbey. The performance was introduced by a Street Singer who sang 'Put off that mask of burning gold' to the tune of 'Finnegan's Wake' and remained on stage throughout the play. William Becker reports that the Abbey actors disliked the paganism in the play, the irreverence towards Yeats and the nonrealistic acting style. Eric Bentley, *The Dramatic Event* (London, 1956), 62; William Becker, 'The Mask Mocked: Or, Farce and the Dialectic of Self,' *Sewanee Review*, 61 (1953): 105.

62 See chapter 1, 3-4.

63 Professor M. C. Bradbrook has called my attention to the correspondence between the medieval Satan's costume and Septimus's feathers. See also 'Leda and the Swan' and 'Alternative Song for the Severed Head' in *The King of the Great Clock Tower*.

64 *Variorum Plays*, 761.

65 *Mythologies*, 326-327; Wade, *Letters*, 512.

66 Rupin W. Desai, *Yeats's Shakespeare* (Evanston, Ill., 1971), 197.

67 Ibid., 3, quoted from 'Reveries over Childhood and Youth' (1915) in *Autobiographies*, ed. Mrs. W. B. Yeats (London, 1961), 29.

68 Worth, *The Irish Drama of Europe from Yeats to Beckett*, 156.

69 Quoted in Ellmann, *The Man and the Masks* (London, 1949), 190.

70 These lines were added to the 1934 edition, emphasizing Decima's self-destruction. See *Variorum Plays*, 753. At that time Yeats was involved in the production of *The King of the Great Clock Tower*, and the revised version, *A Full Moon in March*, both of which bore directly upon his interpretation of *The Player Queen*. See Chapter 5, 86-89, this book.

71 *Explorations*, 250.

72 *Poetry*, March 1913, 126. Pound added that 'it is the presentation of such an image which gives that sudden sense of liberation; that sense of freedom from time and space limits; that sense of sudden growth, which we experience in the presence of the greatest works of art.'

73 *Essays and Introductions*, 235.

74 Fenollosa and Pound, *'Noh' or Accomplishment*, 196. In 1914 Yeats completed the notes and two essays — 'Witches and Wizards and Irish Folklore' and 'Swedenborg, Mediums, and the Desolate Places' — based on the legends he and Lady Gregory had collected. See Lady Gregory, *Visions and Beliefs in the West of Ireland* (London, 1920), which includes Yeats's work.

75 Reprinted in *Literary Essays*, ed. T. S. Eliot (London, 1954), 9.

Notes to pages 61-62

76 Quoted in Earl Miner, *The Japanese Tradition in British and American Literature* (Princeton, 1958), 111. Miner comments on Pound's enthusiasm for Whistler's art, citing Wyndham Lewis: 'Pound's nearest American analogue in the past is not Whitman, ... or Mark Twain, but a painter, James McNeill Whistler.... Like Pound in the literary art, it is in the extreme-orient that Whistler discovered the fundamental adjustments of his preference.' In a letter to Harriet Monroe in 1912, Pound said he counted Whistler as 'our only great artist, and even this informal salute, drastic as it is, may not be out of place at the threshold of what I hope is an endeavor to carry into our American poetry the same sort of life and intensity which he infused into modern painting.' *The Letters of Ezra Pound, 1907-1941*, ed. D. D. Paige (New York, 1950), 10.
77 *Essays and Introductions*, 349.
78 Ibid., 348.
79 Ibid.
80 Ibid., 233. In a note to *At the Hawk's Well*, Yeats again emphasized the importance of the traditional image: 'Shakespeare's art was public, now resounding and declamatory, now lyrical and subtle, but always public, because poetry was a part of the general life of a people who had been trained by the Church to listen to difficult words and who sang, instead of the songs of the music-halls, many songs that are still beautiful.' *Variorum Plays*, 417. For a discussion of Pound's 'Image' and contemporary linguistic theories, see Wallace Martin, 'The Sources of the Imagist Aesthetic,' *PMLA*, 85, no. 2 (March 1970).
81 *Essays and Introductions*, 354-355.

Notes to pages 63-67

CHAPTER 4

1 W. B. Yeats, *A Vision* (London, 1937, rpt. 1961), 28-29.
2 See Walter René Fuerst and Samuel J. Hume, *Twentieth-Century Stage Decoration* (London, 1929), chapter 6: 'Architectural Stages and Permanent Settings'; Robert Speaight, *William Poel and the Elizabethan Revival* (London, 1959); Denis Bablet, *Esthétique Générale du Décor de Théâtre de 1870 à 1914* (Paris, 1965); Peter Arnott, *Greek Scenic Conventions In the Fifth Century B.C.* (Oxford, 1962). Professor Arnott notes that the German archaeological discoveries of Höpken and Dorpfeld in the 1880s and 1890s altered the concept of classical Greek theatre.
3 Craig read the first chapter of Volume II of *The Medieval Stage* several times a year, but disliked the later 'desparate' moralities and mystery plays held outside the church building. Gordon Craig, *Scene* (London, 1923), 6.
4 'Improvements in Stage Scenery,' Patent Number 1771, A.D. 1910. A contemporary critic noted that in 1912, the two major theatre events in London were Granville Barker's production of *The Winter's Tale* and the exhibition of Craig's screens at the Leicester Galleries. Granville Barker remarked that Craig's scenery, especially the 1902 production of *Bethlehem*, taught him to 'detest' excessive scenery. Huntly Carter, *The Theatre of Max Reinhardt* (London, 1914), 291-292.
5 Carter, *The Theatre of Max Reinhardt* (London, 1914), 299.
6 Ibid.
7 Ibid.
8 *The Letters of W. B. Yeats*, ed. Allan Wade (London, 1954), 579. No volume appeared until *Plays and Controversies* (1923), in which Yeats's earlier theatre criticism from *Samhain* was printed with the plays. The events mentioned in the letter occurred in 1911 and 1912: *The Winter's Tale*, 1912; the Russian Ballet's London visit, 1912; Reinhardt's London production of *The Miracle*, 1911; and *Oedipus Rex*, 1912. In a lecture at Harvard on 11 November 1911, Yeats discussed Reinhardt's theatre experiments. E. Engelberg, *The Vast Design* (Toronto, 1964), 80-81.
9 Arnott, *Green Scenic Conventions*, 3-4.
10 Arthur Symons, 'The Ideas of Richard Wagner' (1907) reprinted in Eric Bentley, ed., *The Theory of the Modern Stage: An Introduction to Modern Theatre and Drama* (London, 1968), 311. Wagner objected to the modern opera house which allowed the undemocratic 'threefold and mutually contradictory appeal to the gallery, the pit, and the boxes, "the vulgar, the Philistine, and the exquisite, thrown into one common pot".' ibid, 307.
11 *Essays and Introductions*, ed. Mrs. W. B. Yeats (London, 1961), 99-100.
12 Symons, 'The Ideas of Richard Wagner,' 307, 311. The practice of placing actors in tall shoes was Roman rather than Greek.
13 Gilbert Murray's letter to *The Times*, answering criticism of the

production is reprinted in Carter, *The Theatre of Max Reinhardt*, 221-222.
14 Quoted in ibid., 210.
15 Ibid., 218.
16 Ibid.
17 Ibid, 218-219. In an earlier London production of *The Miracle* Reinhardt had transformed a proscenium theatre into a cathedral.
18 *The Birth of Tragedy and the Case of Wagner*, trans., with Commentary, by Walter Kaufman (New York, 1967), 64-65.
19 Ibid., 62-63. Yeats's reading of Nietzsche clarified his own thought:

Letter of (?) September 26, 1902: 'Nietzsche completes Blake and has the same roots....'
Letter of May 14, 1903: 'The close of the last century was full of a strange desire to get out of form, to get to some kind of disembodied beauty, and now it seems to me the contrary impulse has come. I feel about me and in me an impulse to create form, to carry the realization of beauty as far as possible. The Greeks said that the Dionysiac enthusiasm preceded the Apollonic and that the Dionysiac was sad and desirous, but that the Apollonic was joyful and self sufficient. Long ago I used to define to myself these two influences as the Transfiguration on the Mountain and the Incarnation.' Wade, *Letters*, 379, 402-403.

Ten years after Reinhardt's London production of *Oedipus Rex*, the Victoria and Albert Museum acknowledged the growing interest in theatre of the past in its 1922 exhibition of contemporary stage design. A. Nicoll, *English Drama: 1900-1930* (Cambridge, 1973), 100.
20 See also F. A. C. Wilson on Yeats's *The Cat and the Moon* as a parable of the philosophy of history in *A Vision*. *Yeats's Iconography* (London, 1960), 145-152. The play was written in 1917 and first performed at the Abbey either in 1926 or 1931. Samuel Beckett's Pozzo and Lucky, who resemble the two characters in Yeats's play, have also been connected with an image of historical process: 'Since the early thirties when Hegel's dialectic and Marx's theory of the class struggle began to interest the younger generation in France, the famous image of the pair *"master and servant"* from Hegel's *Phaenomenologie des Geistes*, so deeply engraved itself into the consciousness of those intellectuals born around 1900 that it occupies today the place which the image of *Prometheus* held in the nineteenth century: It has become the *image of man in general*.' Günther Anders, 'Being without Time: On Beckett's Play *Waiting for Godot*,' in Martin Esslin, ed., *Samuel Beckett: A Collection of Critical Essays* (Englewood Cliffs, N.J., 1965), 149.
21 *A Vision*, 27-28.
22 *Collected Plays* (London, 1952), 579.
23 Curtis Bradford, *Yeats at Work* (Carbondale, Pa., 1965), 241. The song is a variation of the theme of Yeats's dance play *Calvary*.
24 In an early prose draft, Yeats worked out this philosophical debate before giving it dramatic shape. Bradford, *Yeats at Work*, 241-245.

25 In an early version, the self-abandonment of the revellers was suggested in 'The Drunken Man's song':

> The Drunken Man's Song
> By dreaming on a crazy drum
> By an odour of spilt blood
> Time's great measure is reversed
> God is drummed out of the tomb.
> (Low sound of drum and rattle)
> The Hebrew. Why are they all suddenly silent and raise their arms above their heads and stand motionless, all their unseeing eyes turned upon this house?
> The Egyptian. There is someone in the room.

Ibid., 248.

26 Yeats wrote, 'It has seemed to me of late that the sense of spiritual reality comes whether to the individual or to crowds from some violent shock, and the idea has the support of tradition.' *Variorum Plays*, 935. The Greek touching the beating heart recalls the opening lyric in which the 'staring virgin' bears away the beating heart of Dionysus. For discussion of Yeats's use of Orphic and Cretan myth and of Tarot symbols, see T.R. Henn, *The Lonely Tower* (London, 1950), 166; Kathleen Raine, *Yeats, the Tarot and the Golden Dawn*, 39-40.

27 Yeats's versions are well known to many audiences. Francis Fergusson based his interpretation of *Oedipus Rex* in *The Idea of a Theatre* on the 1944 production of Yeats's version, with Lawrence Olivier as Oedipus. In 1956, the Stratford Ontario Festival Players under the direction of Tyrone Guthrie presented Yeats's version at the Edinburgh Festival. Guthrie later made the film version based on his highly stylised production.

28 J.M. Hone, *W.B. Yeats: 1865-1939* (London, 1942), 257.

29 Ibid., 256. In 1903, Murray first wrote to Yeats to thank him 'for the extraordinary pleasure which I have received from your Countess Cathleen and Land of Heart's Desire.' (Unpublished letter in the collection of Michael Yeats.) Yeats asked Murray to join him in the short-lived Masquers Society, and he followed all the productions of Euripides which Murray, Granville Barker and Florence Farr staged in London. Murray's description of the Masquers, Mrs Patrick Campbell and Florence Farr complements Yeats's more serious description of their efforts:

> But living in Surrey brought him [Murray] in touch with less serious projects. There was the Theatre of Beauty, about which he was approached by Yeats; he was abroad when the letter reached him, reading Hippolytus scholia in the Naples Museum. 'A preposterous name,' he wrote to his wife, 'Even an offensive name. I shall decline to be on the committee.' But when it emerged a few days later as The Masquers, founded to 'produce only those works which convey a sentiment of beauty,' his name appears, elected apparently in his absence, on a managing committee with Yeats, Sturge Moore and

Notes to pages 75-76

Arthur Symons: Miss Craig their only link with the professional stage, money and experience lacking. 'My hands are red with the life blood of the Masquers,' he was writing soon, dismayed by their wish to do his *Hippolytus*; and 'I felt much the same with modifications about Mrs. Patrick Campbell when she wished to chalk herself over and "do it in the Chinese style".' In this year Florence Farr, whose 'speaking to the psaltery' was so much admired by Yeats, was founding the Fellowship of the Dancers, 'to meet once a month in beautiful and simple dresses'; they were to dance a farandola, to chant Nietzsche, she to chant a chorus from the *Bacchae* — 'my dream for them is to some day do scenes from your Bacchae.' She was Chorus Leader in the two professional productions at the Court Theatre, and then returned to her quest for the *Bacchae*. 'My Bacchae choruses will be very different from anything I was allowed to do at the Court,' she confided to the translators; 'PS Can you let me have the missing parts of the Bacchae restored?' We do not know what he answered.

Gilbert Murray: An Unfinished Autobiography, with Contributions by his Friends, ed. Jean Smith and Arnold Toynbee (London, 1960), 109.

30 Craig's demands that he control any production using his screens and that he personally supervise construction of any masks were often impractical. On one occasion Craig wrote to Yeats from Florence suggesting that the masks being prepared in Dublin for *The Hour-Glass* be posted to him for inspection. The letter, undated, is in Michael Yeats's private collection.

31 'Plain Man's *Oedipus*,' *New York Times* (January 15, 1933), reprinted in Wade, 537. The note continues, 'About five years ago my wife found the manuscript and set me to work again, and when the dialogue was revised and the choruses written, Lady Gregory and I went through it all, altering every sentence that might not be intelligible on the Blasket Islands. Have I made a plain man's *Oedipus*? The pit and gallery of the Abbey Theatre think so.'

32 Letter of Sunday, June 1904, quoted in Ann Saddlemyer, 'Synge to MacKenna: The Mature Years', in Robin Skelton and David Clark, eds., *Irish Renaissance* (Dublin, 1965), 69. Murray's producer Granville Barker also directed the Stage Society's production of Yeats's play, *Where There is Nothing*, later that month.

33 Arnold Dolmetsch, who made Florence Farr's psaltery, had arranged and performed the music for William Poel's Elizabethan productions.

34 Sybil Thorndike in collaboration with Lewis Casson, 'The Theatre and Gilbert Murray' in *Gilbert Murray: An Unfinished Autobiography*, 154. Miss Thorndike, who was in the 1908 *Hippolytus* produced by Lewis Casson, remarks that 'Throughout the controversy and experiment Murray's chief anxieties were his horror of anything approaching the ladylike languor of the Alma Tadema-Albert Moore "Greek" convention of those days, and his insistence on the clarity and intelligibility of the words themselves.' The 1908 Birmingham performance was on an open stage with three levels, with room for elaborate choric movement, ibid., 154, 159-160.

Notes to pages 76-80

35 The importance of the chorus might be altered, Yeats added, if the play is performed in a different sort of theatre: 'A producer who has a space below the level of the stage, where a chorus can move about the altar, may do well to experiment with that old thought of mine and keep his singers as much in the range of the speaking voice as if they sang "The west's awake" or sang round a binnacle.' Yeats referred earlier to 'that old thought of mine' in discussing the songs for the chorus: 'Years ago I persuaded Florence Farr to train the chorus for a Greek play that the sung words were almost as intelligible and dramatic as the spoken; and I have commended that art of hers in *Speaking to the Psaltery*. I asked my Dublin producer Lennox Robinson to disregard that essay.' Preface to *Sophocles' King Oedipus: A Version for the Modern Stage* (London, 1928), v, vi.
36 Ibid., vi.
37 Talk on *King Oedipus* broadcast from Belfast, September 8, 1931. Typescript in Michael Yeats's collection of unpublished manuscripts.
38 Gilbert Murray, *Oedipus King of Thebes by Sophocles* (London, 1911), 27-28.
39 Sir Richard C. Jebb, *The Tragedies of Sophocles Translated into English Prose* (Cambridge, 1904), 108. Yeats worked partly from Jebb's version.
40 In the 1928 publication of *King Oedipus*, the music used in the Abbey production was printed with the note that the final chorus was spoken, not sung, by the Leader. The *New York Times* review, 26 December 1926 notes that 'when the chorus, standing before the closed curtain, spoke the concluding line, "Call no man happy while he lives," there followed a scene of enthusiasm surpassing scenes with which the theatre is dotted.' The use of curtain and concluding song is all similar to the conclusion of *The Land of Heart's Desire, The Hour-Glass* and the dance plays.
41 See especially Yeats's adaptation of the Kommos (*Collected Plays*, 567) and the final episode, 573-575.
42 *The Collected Poems* (London, 1967), 217-218.
43 Ibid., 182-183.
44 *Mythologies*, 341.
45 The group included Gilbert Murray of Oxford and Francis Cornford of Cambridge. For assessments of their work see A. W. Pickard-Cambridge, *Dithyramb, Tragedy and Comedy* (Oxford, 1927); Gerald Else, *The Origin and Early Form of Greek Tragedy* (Cambridge, Mass., 1965) and G. S. Kirk, *Myth: Its Meaning and Functions in Ancient and other Cultures* (Cambridge, 1970).
46 *Ancient Art and Ritual* (London, 1914), 53.
47 Ibid., 25-26. Miss Harrison cites Roger Fry's article, 'An Essay in Aesthetics' (*New Quarterly*, April 1909), which gives a similar view of the function of art. Miss Harrison notes that the theory that ritual preceded myth was first proposed by William Robertson Smith, to whom James Frazer dedicated his first edition (1890) of *The Golden Bough*.

48 Ibid., 26.
49 Ibid., 72-73.
50 Ibid. Miss Harrison refers to Whitehead's book, *Introduction to Mathematics*, chapter 12, 'Periodicity in Nature.' See also Yeats's letters to Mrs Olivia Shakespear: 'I have found a very difficult but profound person Whitehead, who seems to have reached my own conclusions about the ultimate things. He has written down the game of chess and I, like some Italian Prince, have made the pages and the court ladies have it out on the lawn. Not that he would recognise his abstract triumph in my gay rabble.' Yeats explained that, having so far read *Science and the Modern World*, he thought Whitehead's terminology and quantum theory were similar to his own terms in *A Vision*. Wade, *Letters*, 712, 713-714.
51 *Essays and Introductions*, 163.
52 Ibid., 287.
53 *Mythologies*, ed. by Mrs. W. B. Yeats (London, 1959), 352. In 'Discoveries: Second Series,' Yeats wrote that 'Passion and energy when they flow unchecked become rhythmical, they take upon themselves a definite beat.' *Irish Renaissance*, 81. Professor Hough discusses the use of biological rhythm in literature in *An Essay in Criticism* (London, 1966).
54 From 'Ireland After the Revolution,' *On the Boiler*, reprinted in *Variorum Plays*, 899. See also Yeats's Introduction to 'Fighting the Waves,' *Dublin University Magazine*, April-June, 1932: 'Let him translate Greek into Irish and learn that our chariot fighting Red Branch resembled the chariot-fighting Greeks and Trojans; that D'Arbois de Joubainville spent his life in the study of Irish for no other reason; that the sacred grove where Oedipus was carried off by the gods differed in nothing from the groves where, according to Connaught tales, men, women and children were carried off; that Greek literature was founded on a folk belief different but little from that of Ireland; that Roman, like English literature, was founded upon the written word.' *Variorum Plays*, 573.

As Yeats wrote in 'Plain Man's *Oedipus*' (1933), 'When I say intelligible on the Blasket Islands I mean that, being an ignorant man, I may not have gone to Greece through a Latin mist. Greek literature, like old Irish literature, was founded upon belief, not like Latin literature upon documents. No man has ever prayed to or dreaded one of Vergil's nymphs, but when Oedipus at Colonus went into the Wood of the Furies he felt the same creeping in his flesh that an Irish countryman feels in certain haunted woods in Galway and in Sligo.' Wade, *Letters*, 537.
55 BBC Typescript in Michael Yeats's collection of unpublished manuscripts.
56 *Essays and Introductions*, 157-158.
57 *A Vision*, 28.
58 BBC typescript, 4-5.

CHAPTER 5

1 'Introduction: Art is an Attitude,' in Walter Rene Fuerst and Samuel J. Hume, *Twentieth-Century Stage Decoration*, 1 (New York, 1967), xiv, xiii. This illustrated study of modern theatre, widely acclaimed when it was first published in 1929, was based on the authors' tour of European theatres.
  Adolphe Appia, one of the leading stage designers on the Continent, developed an architectural stage setting similar to Gordon Craig's work.
2 Ibid., xiv.
3 *Explorations*, ed. Mrs. W. B. Yeats (London, 1962), 313.
4 *The Letters of W. B. Yeats*, ed. Allan Wade (New York, 1955), 72.
5 When Terence Gray, the Festival Theatre director, visited Athens at the age of 18, he made sketches was the Theatre of Dionysus: 'It is evident that the feature which most interested him was the relationship between the acting area and the first row of seats, for he has pencilled in across the Greek orchestra the relative position of the front stalls of a modern proscenium theatre.' Graham Woodruff, 'Terence Gray and Theatre Design,' *Theatre Research*, 11, nos. 2 and 3 (1971): 118.
6 See also Yeats's description of his 'system' in *A Vision*: '...stylistic arrangements of experience comparable to the cubes in the drawing of Wyndham Lewis and to the Ovoids in the sculpture of Brancusi.' 25.
7 Ninette de Valois, *Come Dance with Me* (London, 1957), 88. The title of the book is taken from Yeats's poem, 'I am of Ireland,' an adaptation of a fourteenth-century poem, *The Irish Dancer*.
8 Wade, *Letters*, 760.
9 *Come Dance with Me*, 89.
10 Fuerst and Hume, *Twentieth-Century Stage Decoration*, xv.
11 I am indebted to Ninette de Valois for this point. For an account of Krop's masks, the Amsterdam production and its effect on Yeats's work, see Liam Miller, *The Noble Drama of W. B. Yeats* (Dublin, 1977), 272-284.
12 From the files of the Macmillan Company New York, *Variorum Plays*, 554.
13 Ibid., 571. Krop's masks were used in the Abbey production. Yeats wrote on 31 July 1929, 'In Dublin they are rehearsing my *Fighting the Waves* with Antheil's music and the Dutch sculptor's masks. The birth of a new art — if one does not make these announcements, one looks so old fashioned.' George Antheil 'promises to keep the instruments required for *The Fighting of the Waves* within the range of the Abbey. During the fight in *Oedipus at Colonus* (he did both plays) there were twelve pianos played at once.' Wade, *Letters*, 765, 760. Antheil later arranged the musical score for Leopold Jessner's productions of the two Oedipus plays at the Berlin Straatstheater in January 1929, with a cast including Lotte Lenya, Helene Weigel, Fritz Kortner, Alexander Granach and Veit Harlan. See John Willett, *Brecht on Theatre* (New York, 1964), 25.
14 Ibid., 530.

15 Ibid., 564. See also Yeats's comment in 1934: 'Europe is changing its philosophy, some four years ago the Russian government silenced the mechanists because social dialectic is impossible if matter is trundled about by some limited force. Certain typical books — *Ulysses*, Mrs. Virginia Woolf's *Waves*, Mr. Ezra Pound's *Draft of XXX Cantos* — suggest a philosophy like that of the *Samkara* school of ancient India, mental and physical objects alike material, a deluge of experience breaking over us and within us, melting limits whether of line or tint; man no hard bright mirror dawdling by the dry sticks of a hedge, but a swimmer, or rather the waves themselves. In this new literature... man in himself is nothing.' *Variorum Plays*, 568-569.
16 Wade, *Letters*, 768.
17 Ibid., 785. In 1932 a similar theatre, the Phoenix, was set up in Dublin. Its ultimate aim 'was that of co-ordinating all the arts, poetry, drama, music, dancing and architecture, which means the evolution of a new form of national drama. This idea is not exactly new as Mr. Yeats had a similar idea in view when he founded the Abbey School of Ballet and he has, in conjunction with this school, successfully experimented with short plays such as *The Only Jealousy of Emer* [*Fighting the Waves*].' J. J. Hayes, 'The Irish Scene,' *Theatre Arts Monthly*, November 1932, 925.
18 BBC Typescript (September 8, 1931) in Michael Yeats's collection of unpublished manuscripts, 6.
19 Robin Skelton and David R. Clark, eds., *Irish Renaissance* (Dublin, 1965), 13-14.
20 *The King of the Great Clock Tower* (Cuala Press, 1934), 22-23.
21 Skelton and Clark, *Irish Renaissance*, 20.
22 Ibid., 23.
23 Ibid. In April, 1933, Yeats wrote, 'This country is exciting. I am told that De Valera has said in private that within three years he will be torn in pieces. It reminds me of a saying by O'Higgins to his wife, 'Nobody can expect to live who has done what I have.' No sooner does a politician get into power than he begins to seek unpopularity. It is the cult of sacrifice planted in the nation by the executions of 1916.' Wade, *Letters*, 80.
24 Skelton and Clark, *Irish Renaissance*, 25.
25 For a detailed discussion of the imagery and Neoplatonic context of the play, see F. A. C. Wilson, *W. B. Yeats and Tradition* (London, 1958), 53-94. For contemporary productions of Wilde's *Salome*, with choreography by Ninette de Valois, see Richard Taylor, *The Drama of W. B. Yeats* (New Haven and London, 1976), 174-175. See also Taylor's view that Yeats violated the delicate balance of earlier dance plays between the subject and the method by over-simplifying the construction of *The King of the Great Clock Tower* while relying wholly on extra-literary modes of production. 175.
26 Quoted in *The Sunday Times*, August 5, 1934, 5. Yeats described the dance in his play as 'more original than I thought it, for when I looked up *Salome* I found that Wilde's dancer never danced with the head in

Notes to pages 89-92

her hands — her dance came before the decapitation of the saint and is a mere uncovering of nakedness. My dance is a long expression of horror and fascination. She first bows before the head (it is on a seat), then in her dance lays it on the ground and dances before it, then holds it in her hands.' Wade, *Letters*, 826.

27 The reviewer noted tha;t the 'atmosphere of Dublin is charged with political dissention.' *The Sunday Times*, 5. The prose version of *The King of the Great Clock Tower* was produced with *The Resurrection*.

28 *The Collected Poems* (London, 1967), 524.

29 *Variorum Plays*, 1311. Yeats's version brings the play closer to Gilbert Murray's interpretation of *Oedipus Rex* as a play based on the old ritual of the daemon and the Earth Mother. See Murray's *Sophocles' Oedipus Rex*, v.

30 See especially the work of George Mills Harper, Kathleen Raine, Philip Sherrard, and F. A. C. Wilson.

31 *Explorations*, 300. Yeats commissioned Michael Scott, a young architect and Abbey player, to design the Peacock Theatre. For a reproduction of the stage plan and discussion of its early years, see Miller, *The Noble Drama of W. B. Yeats*, 267-270.

32 In 1924, the Irish Free State revived the Aonachy Tailteann, and in 1928 drama was included among the competitions which were opened in 1931 to all amateur groups of Irish descendants. The judges included Dudley Digges of the New York Theatre Guild, Nugent Monck of the Norwich Maddermarket Theatre, and William Armstrong of the Liverpool Playhouse. Similar to the earlier Abbey programmes of mixed plays (see chapter III, 36), the competition required each group 'to present two plays of contrasting character, that is, a tragedy or drama, and a comedy, and the whole performance to make up a full evening's entertainment lasting not more than three hours. The plays, left to each group's own selection, ranged from works of the Abbey school to plays of Spanish, English and American authorship,' Hayes, 'Who will go to Ireland for Aonachy Tailteann?,' *Theatre Arts Monthly* (January 1931), 78-80. See also Allardyce Nicoll on the growth of festivals in England. In August, 1929, there were both the Malvern Festival, dedicated to G. B. Shaw, and the Canterbury Festival, both inspired by Max Reinhardt's Salzburg Festival. *English Drama: 1900-1930* (Cambridge, 1973), 91-93.

33 'The English Scene: Then and Now,' *Theatre Arts Monthly*, September 1932, 700-701.

34 'The Scene in England: Current Plays — A Small Professional Theatre,' *Theatre Arts Monthly*, March 1934, 176.

35 'The London Scene: The Principle of Selectivity,' *Theatre Arts Monthly*, January 1931, 22.

36 Norman Marshall, *The Other Theatre* (London, 1947), 149. After leaving Diaghilev's Russian Ballet in 1926, Ninette de Valois started a School of Choreographical Art in Kensington and did some work for the Festival Theatre, Cambridge. In 1927 she set up the Abbey School of Ballet, and in 1930 she helped to establish the Camargo Society, which

was disbanded two years later when its aims had been achieved: to create an interest in English dancers, to give an opportunity for the work of Sir Frederick Ashton and Ninette de Valois, to persuade composers and painters to take a serious interest in ballet and to prepare the way for the Vic-Wells Ballet and the Rambert Company. For a discussion of her work in London, see ibid., 83.

37   Yeats wrote to the actress Margot Ruddock, 'I am rewriting *The King of the Great Clock Tower* giving the Queen a speaking part, that you may act it. I have so arranged it that you can give place to a dancer (quite easy as you will both wear masks). The old version of the play is bad because abstract and incoherent. This version is poignant and simple — lyrical dialogue all simple. It takes years to get my plays right.' Roger McHugh, ed., *Ah, Sweet Dancer: W. B. Yeats, Margot Ruddock* (London, 1970), 23. At that time Yeats was attending the Allesandro Volta Congress in Rome. Invited by Pirandello to give a lecture on the Abbey Theatre, he joined Craig, Maeterlinck, Tairov, Marinetti, Gropius and others in discussions of contemporary theatre. For a contemporary account of the Congress, covering topics such as the relation of dramatic art to film, radio and stadium sport, theatre architecture, theatre in the moral life of the nation, and state assistance to theatre, see Ashley Dukes, 'The Scene in Europe: A Roman Theatre Congress,' *Theatre Arts Monthly*, December, 1934, 905-910. Yeats's talk, 'The Irish National Theatre,' is printed in *Convegno di Lettere 8-14 Octobre 1934-XII. Tema: Il Teatro Drammatico* (Rome, 1935), 13: 386-392. See also extracts of the talk in Miller, *The Noble Art of W. B. Yeats*, 297-299.

38   McHugh, *Ah, Sweet Dancer*, 11.

39   On the death of Diaghilev, Doone left the Russian Ballet to train as a choreographer and producer. While acting at the Cambridge Festival Theatre he met Tyrone Guthrie and the idea of the Group Theatre was first discussed. Established in 1932 for the production of ancient and modern plays, the company published its aims in a programme leaflet, January 1934: 'It is a permanent GROUP of actors, painters, singers, dancers, and members of the audience, who do everything and do it together, and are thus creating a theatre representative of the spirit today.' Doone served as producer, choreographer and dancer for the Group, whose productions included W. H. Auden's *The Dance of Death* in February 1934 (dedicated to the founders of the Group Theatre, produced by Doone and Guthrie, with Doone dancing the role of Death with a mask by Henry Moore; T. S. Eliot's *Sweeney Agonistes* in October 1935 (in a programme note, Doone describes Sweeney as 'a modern Orestes'); Louis MacNeice's adaptation of *Agamemnon* in November 1936 (with music by Benjamin Britten and masks by Robert Medley); the Auden-Isherwood plays, *The Dog Beneath the Skin*, Autumn 1935, *The Ascent of F6*, February 1937, *On the Frontier*, 1938; Louis MacNeice's own play, *Out of the Picture*, December 1937 (done in the manner of the Auden-Isherwood plays and produced by Doone with music by Britten). The programmes of the Group Theatre

Notes to pages 93-94

Company at the Westminster Theatre are in the Enthoven Collection at the Victoria and Albert Museum in London. For a discussion of the similarities between Yeats's dance plays and the work of the Group Theatre Company, see Katharine Worth, *The Irish Drama of Europe from Yeats to Beckett*, 211-212.

40 McHugh, *Ah, Sweet Dancer*, 34-35.
41 From T. S. Eliot's letter to Rubert Doone, which continues: 'Obviously it is impossible for any one man to produce fine plays in the time at your disposal. I am afraid that the whole thing has been badly muddled. Whether the issue would have been more successful had Yeats been able to be in London I do not know.... I'm sorriest on account of Auden, and hope you will be able to make arrangements with the Westminster Theatre to give him a show in the autumn.' E. Martin Browne, *The Making of T. S. Eliot's Plays* (Cambridge, 1970), 39-40. See also Yeats's comment that he doubted whether Ashley Dukes would produce *The Player Queen*. Wade, *Letters*, 835.
42 'The British Isles,' *Theatre Arts Monthly*, April 1939, 252.
43 The Yeats Festival had a varied reception, due in part to the unfinished state of the productions. The reviewer in the *Observer*, 3 November 1935, pointed out that when paying a compliment to a major poet, 'skilful preparation should be one of the first considerations in making [the plays] acceptable.' *The Player Queen* provoked the widest range of critical response, from the *Times* ('It shows forth the sublime mystery of vocation, in the woman basely born but dowered with queenliness.'), to the *Evening Standard* ('The plays are of the kind usually performed by the torch-bearing enthusiasts who cultivate the Higher Drama and are always moving toward something or other.')
44 M. C. Bradbrook, *Ibsen the Norwegian* (London, 1946), 125.
45 While correcting the proofs for *The Collected poems* in June 1932, Yeats wrote that he was amazed to find always the same themes — a denunciation of old age and the complementary figures of the swordsman and the saint: 'The swordsman throughout repudiates the saint, but not without vacillation. Is that perhaps the sole theme — Usheen and Patrick — "so get you gone Von Hügel though with blessings on your head"?' Wade, *Letters*, 798. See also Richard Taylor's discussion of *The Herne's Egg* in *The Drama of W. B. Yeats*, 179-187.
46 Wade, *Letters*, 836. During the composition of *The Herne's Egg*, Yeats was working with Shri Purohit Swami on an English version of *The Ten Principal Upanishads*. See also Yeats's letter, 'Shri Purohit Swami is with me, and the play is his philosophy in a fable, or mine confirmed by him.' 844.
47 Worth, *The Irish Drama of Europe from Yeats to Beckett*, 193. See also her excellent discussion of London theatre and dance in the 1970s in 'The Vitality of the Yeatsian Theatre,' 194-219.
48 Taylor, *The Drama of W. B. Yeats*, 186-187. For an account of Yeats's theatre in relation to the work of Antonin Artaud, Jerzy Grotowski, Peter Brook, the North American troupes of the 1960s, and the noted Yeats productions by the Cafe La Mama in New York and Le Theatre

d'Aran in Paris, see James W. Flannery, *W. B. Yeats and the Idea of a Theatre: The Early Abbey Theatre in Theory and Practice* (Toronto, 1976), 367-375. For an account of the influence of Yeats's dance plays on the Little Theatre Movement in Japan, see Shotaro Oshima, *W. B. Yeats and Japan, In his Relation with the Zen Philosophy and the 'Noh'* (Tokyo, 1964), 14-16. Professor Oshima has pointed out to me that Michio Itoh, who danced the original hawk dance in 1916 and produced *At the Hawk's Well* in Japan in 1939, was admired by Yeats for his philosophical mind which was reflected in his style of dance. I am grateful to Professor Oshima for allowing me to see his unpublished lecture on Japanese theatre, 'Between Shapes and Shadows,' which includes passages from Itoh's book, *A Room for Those Who Wish to Become Beautiful* (Tokyo, 1956).

The extent of T. S. Eliot's famous praise of Yeats's drama in "Yeats [The first annual Yeats Lecture, delivered to the Friends of the Irish Academy at the Abbey Theatre in 1940],' reprinted in *On Poetry and Poets* (London, 1957), is highlighted by pages from a sketchbook in the collection of Eliot manuscripts at Magdalene College, Cambridge. Two pages are filled with notes for the Yeats lectures, the reverse sides of which include a draft of his portrait of Yeats in the second part of 'Little Gidding.'

49 *Explorations*, 333, 448.
50 T. R. Henn, 'Yeats and the Theatre,' in Francis Warner, ed., *Studies in the Arts* (Oxford, 1968), 80.
51 *Variorum Plays*, 569-570. See also Yeats's letter in 1929 that Frobenius 'has confirmed a conception I have had for many years, a conception that has freed me from British liberalism and all its dreams. The one heroic sanction is that of the last battle of the Norse Gods. Of a gay struggle without hope.' *W. B. Yeats and T. Sturge Moore: Their Correspondence 1901-1937*, ed. Ursula Bridges (London, 1953), 154.
52 Wade, *Letters*, 913. The Festival included productions of Synge's *The Well of the Saints, Riders to the Sea, The Playboy of the Western World*, Yeats's *On Baile's Strand, Purgatory, Cathleen ni Houlihan*, Lady Gregory's *The Rising of the Moon*, and Shaw's *The Shewing up of Blanco Posnet*. For a review of the Festival see Una Ellis-Fermor, 'Dramatic Notes,' *English*, II 9 (1938), 174-177.
53 *Explorations*, 339-340.

Select Bibliography

There are several complete bibliographies of Yeats, including *A Bibliography of the Writings of W. B. Yeats*, edited by Allen Wade, third edition revised and edited by Russell K. Alspach (London, 1968); *A Bibliography of Yeats Criticism 1887-1965*, edited by K. G. W. Cross and R. T. Dunlop (London, 1971); *W. B. Yeats's Plays: An Annotated Check-list of Criticism,* edited by K. P. S. Jochum (Saarbrücken, 1966); and the annual *PMLA* bibliographies. The following list is intended as a brief guide. I have listed the books, articles, theses and unpublished material which I have found useful in the study of Yeats and modern theatre.

BOOKS

Abel, Lionel, *Métathéâtre: A New View of Dramatic Form* (New York, 1963).
Artaud, Antonin, *The Theatre and its Double*, trans. Mary Caroline Richards (New York, 1958).
Aylen, Leo, *Greek Tragedy and the Modern World* (London, 1964).
Bablet, Denis, *Esthétique générale du décor de théâtre de 1870 à 1914* (Paris, 1965).
Bablet, Denis, and Jacquot, Jean, *Le Lieu théatral dans la société moderne* (Paris, 1963).
Bablet, Denis, *La Mise en scène contemporaine, I: 1887-1914* (Paris, 1968).
Bell, Stanley, Marshall, Norman, and Southern, Richard, *Essentials of Stage-Planning* (London, 1949).
Bentley, Eric, *In Search of Theatre* (London, 1954).

Bentley, Eric, *The Dramatic Event* (London, 1956).
Bieber, Margarete, *The History of Greek and Roman Theatre* (with a final chapter on modern productions) (Princeton and Oxford, 1939, 1961).
Blythe, Ernest, *The Abbey Theatre* (Dublin, n.d.)
Bornstein, George, *Yeats and Shelley* (Chicago and London, 1970).
Craig, Gordon, *Woodcuts and Some Words* (London, 1924).
Desai, Rupin W., *Yeats's Shakespeare* (Evanston, Illinois, 1971).
Fallon, Gabriel, *The Abbey and the Actor* (Dublin, 1969).
Flannery, James W., *W. B. Yeats and the Idea of a Theatre: The Early Abbey Theatre in Theory and Practice* (Toronto, 1976).
Fletcher, Ian, and Gordon, D.J. (eds.), *W. B. Yeats: Images of a Poet* (Manchester, 1961).
Friedman, Barton R., *Adventures in the Deeps of the Mind: The Cuchulain Cycle of W. B. Yeats* (Princeton, 1977).
Henn, T. R., *The Harvest of Tragedy* (London, 1954, 1966).
Holloway, Joseph, *Joseph Holloway's Abbey Theatre, A Selecrion from his Unpublished Journal, Impressions of a Dublin Playgoer*, ed. Robert Hogan and Michael J. O'Neill (Carbondale, 1967).
Leeper, Janet, *Edward Gordon Craig: Designs for the Theatre* (London, 1948).
MacLiammoir, Michael and Boland, Eavan, *W. B. Yeats and his World* (London, 1971).
McHugh, Rober (ed.), *Ah, Sweet Dancer: W. B. Yeats, Margot Ruddock* (London, 1970).
Miller, Liam, *The Noble Drama of W. B. Yeats* (Dublin, 1977).
Moore, John Rees, *Masks of Love and Death: Yeats as Dramatist* (Ithaca, N.Y. and London, 1971).
Nicoll, Allardyce, *English Drama: 1900-1930* (Cambridge, 1973).
O'Casey, Sean, *Inishfallen Fare Thee Well* (London, 1949).
O'Driscoll, Robert and Reynolds, Lorna (eds), *Yeats and the Theatre* (London and Toronto, 1975).
Qamber, Akhtar, *Yeats and the Noh* (New York and Tokyo, 1974).
Raine, Kathleen, *Yeats, the Tarot and the Golden Dawn* (Dublin, 1972).

Select Bibliography

Saul, George Brandon, *Prolegomena to the Study of Yeats's Plays* (Philadelphia and London, 1958).
Skene, Reg., *The Cuchulain Plays of W.B. Yeats* (London, 1974).
Taylor, Richard, *The Drama of W.B. Yeats: Irish Myth and the Japanese Nō* (New Haven and London, 1976).
Ussher, Arland, *The Twenty Two Keys of the Tarot* (Dublin, 1953, 1969).
Worth, Katharine, *The Irish Drama of Europe from Yeats to Beckett* (London, 1978).
Ze-Ami's Kadensho, trans. Chuichi, SaKuRai and others (Tokyo, 1968).

ARTICLES

Anon., 'Memorable first night' (a review of the Abbey productions of *The Resurrection* and *The King of the Great Clock Tower*), *Sunday Times*, 5 August 1934, p. 5.
Anon., 'Mr. Yeats at the Abbey Theatre', *The Irish Times*, 9 September 1911, p. 8.
Becker, William, 'The mask mocked: or, farce and the dialectic of self', *Sewanee Review*, LXI, 1953, 82-103.
Bentley, Eric, 'On staging Yeats's plays', *New Republic*, CXXVIII, 15 June 1953, 17-18.
Bottomley, Gordon, 'Charles Ricketts R.A.', *Arts Theatre Monthly*, May 1932, 377-95.
Bushrui, S.B., '"The Hour-Glass": Yeats's revisions, 1903-1922', *W.B. Yeats: Centenary Essays on the Art of W.B. Yeats* ed. D.E.S. Maxwell and S.B. Bushrui (Ibadan, 1965), pp. 189-216.
C.P.C., 'Dramatic notes: Oedipus at the Abbey', *The Irish Statesman*, 11 December 1926, p. 326.
Colum, Padraic, 'Poet's progress: W.B. Yeats in the theatre' (a review of *The Collected Plays*), *Theatre Arts Monthly*, December 1935, pp. 936-43).
Craig, Gordon, 'The Actor and the Über-Marionette', reprinted in *On the Art of the Theatre* (London, 1957).
Craig, Gordon, 'Is poetic drama born again?', *The Mask*, V, 1912-13, p. 291.

Dukes, Ashley, 'The English scene: then and now', *Theatre Arts Monthly*, September 1932, pp. 698-704.
Dukes, Ashley, 'The scene in Europe: a Roman theatre congress', *Theatre Arts Monthly*, December 1934, pp. 905-10.
Dukes, Ashley, 'The British Isles', *Theatre Arts Monthly*, April 1939, pp. 252-6.
Ellis-Fermor, Una, 'Dramatic notes' (a review of the Abbey Festival, August 1938), *English*, II, **9**, 1938, pp. 174-7.
Fay, William, 'The poet and the actor', *Scattering Branches*, ed. Stephen Gwynn (London, 1940).
Hayes, J. J., 'Who will go to Ireland for Aonachy Tailteann?', *Theatre Arts Monthly*, January 1931, pp. 78-80.
Hayes, J. J., 'The Irish scene', *Theatre Arts Monthly*, November 1932, pp. 922-6.
Henn, T. R. 'Yeats and the theatre', *Studies in the Arts*, ed. Francis Warner (Oxford, 1968), pp. 62-81.
Henn, T. R., 'Towards the values', *The Southern Review*, NS 5.2, 1969, pp. 833-49.
Leach, Wilford, 'Music for words perhaps [a new instrument and a full score, composed for the spoken voice, of Yeats's *King Oedipus*]', *Theatre Arts*, January 1953, pp. 65-8.
McHugh, Roger (ed.), *Threshold* (issues on Yeats's theatre), 19, Autumn 1965).
Mead, G. R. S., 'The Sacred dance of Jesus', *The Quest*, II, **1**, October 1910, pp. 45-67.
Miller, Liam, 'W. B. Yeats and stage design at the Abbey Theatre', *Malahat Review*, 16, 1970, pp. 50-64 (followed by twenty pages of illustrations).
Parkinson, Thomas, 'The later plays of W. B. Yeats', *Modern Drama: Essays in Criticism*, ed. T. Bogard and W. I. Oliver (New York, 1965), pp. 385-93).
Pearce, Donald R., 'Yeats's last plays: an interpretation', *Journal of English Literary History*, XVIII, 1 March 1951, pp. 67-76.
Pitkin, William, 'Stage designs, masks and costumes for plays of W. B. Yeats', *Bard Review*, April 1949, pp. 93-110.
Robinson, Lennox, 'The man and the dramatist', *Scattering Branches*, ed. Stephen Gwynn (London, 1940).
Rothenstein, Sir William, 'Yeats as a painter saw him', ibid.

Saddlemyer, Ann, '"The Noble and the Beggar-Man": Yeats and literary nationalism', *The World of W. B. Yeats: Essays in Perspective*, ed. Robin Skelton and Ann Saddlemyer (Dublin, 1965), pp. 22- 39).

Saddlemyer, Ann, '"Worn Out with Dreams": Dublin's Abbey Theatre', ibid., pp. 104-32.

Starkie, Walter, 'W. B. Yeats and the Abbey Theatre', *The Southern Review*, NS 5.2, 1969, pp. 886-921.

Stucki, Yasuko, 'Yeats's drama and the Nō: a comparative study in dramatic theories', *Modern Drama*, LX, May 1966, pp. 101-22.

Thwaite, Anthony, 'Yeats and the Noh', *The Twentieth Century*, CLXII, 1959, pp. 235-42.

Tsukimura, Reiko, 'A comparison of Yeats's *At the Hawk's Well* and its Noh version, *Taka no izumi*', *Literature, East and West*, XI, **4**, December 1967, pp. 385-97.

Yeats, W. B., An interview given to *Hearth and Home*, *The Mask*, VII, 1914, p. 141.

THESES

Becker, William, 'Yeats as a playwright', PhD Thesis, Oxford University, 1953.

Cole, Alan, 'Stagecraft in the modern Dublin theatre', PhD Thesis, Trinity College, Dublin, 1954.

Flannery, James William, 'W. B. Yeats and the idea of a theatre: the early Abbey Theatre in theory and practice', PhD Thesis, Trinity College, Dublin, 1970.

UNPUBLISHED MATERIAL

Craig, Gordon, Stage designs and letters to W. B. Yeats, in Michael Yeats's possession.

Eliot, T. S., First draft of Yeats lecture and of the second section of 'Little Gidding', among the Eliot manuscripts at Magdalene College, Cambridge.

Murray, Gilbert, Letters and telegrams to W. B. Yeats, in Michael Yeats's possession.

Oshima, Shotaro, 'Between shapes and shadows', unpublished lecture delivered in Canada, 1973.

Yeats, W. B., Talk on *Oedipus the King*, to be broadcast from Belfast, 8 September 1931, typescript in Michael Yeats's possession.

Sources of Illustrations

1 Liam Miller, W. B. Yeats and Stage Design at the Abbey Theatre, *Malahat Review*, Vol. 16 (1970), Plate 3.
2 Richard Southern, *The Victorian Theatre*, (Newton Abbot, 1970), 8-9.
3 (a) Sebastiano Serlio, *Tutte L'Opere d'Architettura et Prospetiva* (Venice, 1619), reprinted Farnborough, 1964, II, 46.
 (b) Edward Craig, *Gordon Craig* (London, 1968), 236.
4 Edward Craig, *Gordon Craig*, 232.
5 Edward Craig, *Gordon Craig*, 289.
6 Liam Miller, *The Noble Art of W. B. Yeats* (Dublin, 1977). 81.
7 Robert O'Driscoll and Lorna Reynolds, eds., *Yeats and the Theatre* (Macmillan of Canada, 1975), Plate 5.
8 Janet Leeper, *Edward Gordon Craig* (London 1948), Plate 22.
9 Denis Bablet, *Esthétique générale du décor de théâtre de 1870 à 1914* (Paris, 1965), Plate 142.
10 Janet Leeper, *Edward Gordon Craig*, 23.
11 W. B. Yeats, *Plays for an Irish Theatre* (London, 1911) between 64 and 65.
12 Liam Miller, 'W. B. Yeats and Stage Design at the Abbey Theatre,' Plate 4.
13 Liam Miller, 'W. B. Yeats and Stage Design at the Abbey Theatre,' Plate 10.
14 Ian Fletcher and D. J. Gordon, eds., *W. B. Yeats: Images of a Poet* (Manchester, 1961), Plate 19.
15 W. B. Yeats, *Four Plays for Dancers* (London, 1921), 4.
16 Ian Fletcher and D. J. Gordon, *W. B. Yeats: Images of a Poet*, Plate 23.
17 Janet Leeper, *Edward Gordon Craig*, Plate 14.

18 Janet Leeper, *Edward Gordon Craig,* Plate 31.
19 Janet Leeper, *Edward Gordon Craig,* Plate 28.
20 Janet Leeper, *Edward Gordon Craig,* Plate 25.
21 Janet Leeper, *Edward Gordon Craig,* Plate 19.
22 Denis Bablet, *Esthétique générale du décor de théâtre de 1870 à 1914,* Plate 174.
23 Denis Bablet, *Esthétique générale du décor de théâtre de 1870 à 1914,* Plate 176.
24 *Theatre Research,* 4-5(1962-63), between 122 and 123.
25 G. A. Duncan, *Abbey Theatre in Pictures* (Dublin, 1963), 13.
26 *Theatre Arts Monthly* (March, 1927), 216.
27 Norman Marshall, *The Other Theatre* (London, 1947), between 64 and 65.
28 Liam Miller, 'W. B. Yeats and Stage Design at the Abbey Theatre,' Plate 1.
29 Ian Fletcher and D. J. Gordon, *W. B. Yeats: Images of a Poet,* Plate 175.
30 Walter René Feurst and Samuel J. Hume, *Twentieth-Century Stage Decoration,* Vol. II (New York, 1929, rpt. 1967), Plate 327.
31 Eric Bentley, *In Search of Theatre* (London, 1954), Plate 23.
32 *Theatre Arts Monthly* (March, 1934), 174.

Acknowledgements

I should like to thank Senator Michael Yeats for allowing me to see unpublished letters, manuscripts, photographs, and sketchbooks, and Ninette de Valois for discussing with me her work with Yeats and the dance plays. I am grateful to Shotaro Oshima for a copy of his unpublished lecture on Japanese classical drama, and J. A. W. Bennett for allowing me to see a manuscript of T. S. Eliot given to Magdalene College, Cambridge. I should also like to thank the American Association of University Women for a fellowship (1971-1972), which enabled me to complete the research for this study, and acknowledge the help of the librarians and staff at the Cambridge University Library; the Bodleian Library, Oxford; Trinity College, Dublin; the British School at Athens; and the Enthoven Theatre Collection at the Victoria and Albert Museum, London. I should also like to thank Girton College, Cambridge, for a grant from their Publications Fund. I have benefitted greatly from discussions with the late T. R. Henn, M. C. Bradbrook, John Northam, David R. Clark, Denis Donoghue and Raymond Williams.

I am grateful to Macmillan of Canada for permission to include chapter 2, originally published in Robert O'Driscoll and Lorna Reynolds, eds., *Yeats and the Theatre* (1975), and to Oxford University Press for permission to include chapter 4, originally published in *Theatre Research International* (May 1976).

Acknowledgements are made to Mr. Michael B. Yeats, Miss Anne Yeats and Macmillan, London, Limited for permission to quote from the works of W. B. Yeats, and to Mr. Michael B. Yeats and Miss Anne Yeats for permission to reproduce illustrations from the Yeats Estate.

Players and Painted Stage

Further acknowledgements are due to Macmillan Publishing Company for permission to reprint extracts from the following: *Explorations* (Copyright © Mrs. W. B. Yeats 1962); *Autobiography* (Copyright 1916, 1936 by Macmillan Publishing Co., Inc., renewed 1944, 1964 by Bertha Georgie Yeats); *Mythologies* (includes selection from *Per Amica Silentia Lunae*) — © Mrs. W. B. Yeats 1959; *A Vision* (Copyright 1937 by W. B. Yeats, renewed 1965 by Bertha Georgie Yeats and Anne Butler Yeats); *Collected Poems* (copyright 1918, 1928, 1933 by Macmillan Publishing Co., Inc., renewed 1946, 1956, 1961 by Bertha Georgie Yeats. Copyright 1940 by Georgie Yeats, renewed 1968 by Bertha Georgie Yeats, Michael Butler Yeats and Anne Yeats); *The Letters of W. B. Yeats* edited by Allan Wade (Copyright 1953, 1954 by Anne Butler Yeats); *The Variorum Edition of the Plays of W. B. Yeats* edited by Russell K. Alspach (Copyright © Russell K. Alspach and Georgie Yeats 1966. Copyright © Macmillan & Co. Ltd. 1965).

Index

'A.E.', 98 n 15
Abbey Theatre, x, xi, 2-4, 7, 11-12, 13, 60, 63, 75-6, 102 n 36
Abbey Company, 11, 34, 36, 56, 75, 86
Abbey School of Ballet, 84-5, 91, 122 n 17
Abbey Second Company, 12, 18, 34-5, 74, 86
Absurd, Theatre of the, 94
Anders, Günther, 116 n 20
Antheil, George, 86, 121 n 13
Antoine, André, 99 n 30
Aonachy Tailteann (Irish amateur drama competition), 91, 123 n 32
Appia, Adolphe, 83, 84, 121 n 1
Archer, William, 101 n 23, 102 n 46
Arnott, Peter, 115 n 2
Artaud, Antonin, 109 n 18, 125 n 48
Ashton, Frederick, 93, 124 n 36
Auden, W. H., 93, 124 n 39, 125 n 41
Awoi no Uye, 44-5, 60

Bablet, Denis, 100 n 5, 115 n 2
Baker, Paul, 111 n 41
Ballet Russe (see Russian Ballet)

Barker, Harley Granville, xi, 63, 65, 67, 101 n 18, 106 n 92, 115 n 4, 117 n 29, 118 n 32
Bayreuth (see Richard Wagner)
Becker, William, 97 n 13, 113 n 61
Beckett, Samuel, 94, 116 n 20
Bentley, Eric, 102 n 36, 113 n 61
Blake, William, 4, 61, 103 n 62, 110 n 28, 111 n 38
Bloom, Harold, 109 n 15
Bornstein, George, 97 n 12, 98 n 18, 109 n 14
Bottomley, Gordon, 108 n 11
Bradbrook, M. C., 113 n 63, 125 n 44
Bradford, Curtis, xiii, 112 n 58, 116 n 23-4, 117 n 25
Brecht, Bertolt, 110 n 26
Brook, Peter, 125 n 48
Browne, Martin E., 93
Burke, Kenneth, 14
Bushrui, S. B., 103 n 54

Camargo Society, 92, 123 n 36
Cambridge Festival Theatre (see Festival Theatre, Cambridge)
Campbell, Mrs Patrick, 58, 117 n 29
Carter, Huntly, 115 n 4
Chambers, E. K., 64

Clark, David R., xii, xiii, 98 n19
Colum, Padraic, 107 n1
Corkery, Daniel, 97 n11
Cornford, Francis, 119 n45
Covent Garden Theatre, London, 67, 75
Craig, Edith, 15, 101 n18, 118 n29
Craig, Edward, 100 n16, 101 n29, 101 n31
Craig, Gordon, ix-x, xi, 1, 12, 13-18, 23, 24-5, 33-5, 56, 57, 59, 60, 64-5, 74-5, 83, 91, 100 n16, 101 n21, 101 n27-31, 102 n36, 102 n43, 105 n91-106 n93, 115 n4, 124 n37
  'The Actor and the Über-Marionette', 48, 105 n87
  'Aeneas and Dido', 13
  The Mask, 23, 26, 33, 35, 101 n27, 103 n54, 103 n59, 105 n91
  On the Art of the Theatre, 103 n62
  'A Note on Marionnettes', 111 n38
  Towards a New Theatre, 33
Craig, May, 113 n59

Dante Alighieri, 30
Desai, Rupin, 58, 109 n16, 113 n66
Diaghilev, Serge de (see also Russian Ballet), xi, 16, 101 n21
Dolmetsch, Arnold, 118 n33
Doone, Rupert, 93, 124 n39
Duggan, G.C., 104 n77
Dukes, Ashley, 91-3, 124 n37
Dulac, Edmund, ix, 93

Easter Uprising, Dublin 1916, 54, 81, 88
Eliade, Mircea, 104 n79
Eliot, T.S., 55, 93, 94, 124 n39, 125 n41, 126 n48
Elizabethan theatre architecture, 64
Ellis-Fermor, Una, 97 n1, 105 n82, 126 n52
Ellmann, Richard, 102 n40, 104 n75, 108 n7, 110 n28, 113 n69
Else, Gerald, 119 n45
Engelberg, Edward, 103 n62, 115 n8
Euripides, 76, 118 n29, 118 n34
Evans, Edith, 112 n59

Fallon, Gabrielle, 99 n30
Farr, Florence, 16, 76, 117 n29, 118 n33, 119 n35
Fay brothers, William and Frank, 2, 11, 15, 98 n30, 100 n16, 102 n43
Fenollosa, Ernest, xiii, 35, 107 n5
— manuscript on Noh drama (edited by Ezra Pound), xiii, 35-7, 40, 41, 54, 55, 110 n26
Fergusson, Francis, 117 n27
Festival Theatre, Cambridge, x, 83-4, 91, 92, 121 n5, 124 n39
Flannery, James W., xiii, 97 n1, 102 n35, 107 n4, 112 n59, 126 n48
Frank Lloyd Wright Theatre, Dallas, Texas, 111 n41
Frazer, James, 119 n47
Friedman, Barton R., 6, 98 n18-26, 100 n15, 102 n43, 109 n14, 109 n16, 111 n38
Fry, Roger, 119 n47

Index

Fuerst, Walter René and Samuel J. Hume, 115 n2, 121 n1

Galsworthy, John, 97 n13
Godwin, E.W., x, 64
Goodwin, K.L., 108 n7
Gordon, D.J., 108 n6
Granville-Barker, Harley (see Barker, Harley Granville)
Gray, Terence, 121 n5
Greek theatre architecture, 64, 76; German theories of, 66, 115 n2
Gregory, Augusta, Lady, 2, 4, 11, 14, 16, 18, 45, 54, 107 n3, 113 n74, 118 n31
Gregory, Robert, ix, 5, 106 n92
Gropius, Walter, 124 n37
Grotowski, Jerzy, 125 n48
Group Theatre Company, London, 124 n39
Guthrie, Tyrone, 117 n27, 124 n39

Harper, George Mills, xiii, 123 n30
Harrison, Jane, 64, 74, 79-80
Harvey, Martin, 105 n91
Hauptmann, 1, 12
Hayes, J.J., 122 n17, 123 n32
Henn, T.R., 24, 94, 103 n55, 117 n26
Herkomer, Hubert von, 100 n16
Holloway, Joseph, 102 n36, 107 n4, 113 n59
Horniman, Annie, 2, 12
Hough, Graham, 120 n53
Housman, Lawrence, 15

IRA (see W.B. Yeats, *The Dreaming of the Bones*), 54, 87-8
Ibsen, Henrik, xi, 1, 3, 12, 93, 101 n23
Imagism, 61, 114 n80
Irish Civil War, Ireland 1922, 82
Irish Literary Theatre, 13
Irving, Henry, 58, 104 n64
Isherwood, Christopher, 124 n39
Itoh, Michio, ix, 84, 126 n48

Japanese Noh drama, xi, xiii, 13, 33, 35-7, 41-3, 50, 60, 74, 95, 107 n5
John, Augustus, 105 n91
Johnson, Lionel, 4
Joyce, James, 87

Kirk, G.S., 119 n45
Krop, Hildo, x, 84, 86, 121 n11, 121 n13

Langer, Susanne K., xii
Leeper, Janet, 101 n21
Little Theatre, London (Yeats Festival), 93

MacKenna, Stephen, 76
MacNeice, Louis, 124 n39
Maddermarket Theatre, Norwich, 107 n3
Maeterlinck, Maurice, 4, 15, 124 n37
Marinetti, Filippo, 124 n37
Marshall, Norman, 1
Martin, Graham, 108 n8
Martin, Wallace, 114 n80
The Mask (see Gordon Craig)
Mayhew, George P., xiii
McHugh, Roger, 124 n37

139

Mead, G.R.S., 112 n48
Mercury Theatre, London, x, 91-3
Miller, Liam, xiii, 98 n16, 102 n35-6, 106 n93, 112 n59, 121 n11, 123 n31, 124 n37
Miner, Earl, 114 n76
Monck, Nugent, 34-5, 107 n3, 123 n32
Moore, George, 3, 102 n46
Moore, John Rees, xiii
Moore, T. Sturge, 15-16, 118 n29
Morris, William, 14
Moscow Art Theatre, 59, 101 n28
Murray, Gilbert, xi, 63, 66, 74-5, 77, 117 n29, 119 n45, 123 n29

Nakamura, Yasuo, 110 n25
naturalism, xi, xii, 1-3, 17, 55, 60, 86, 97 n1
Nicoll, Allardyce, 106 n91, 116 n19, 123 n32
Nietzsche, Frederick, 15, 68, 74, 98 n26, 116 n19, 118 n29
Nishikigi, 54-5
Noh (see Japanese Noh drama)

O'Casey, Sean, 54, 87, 94
O'Connor, Frank, 99 n30, 103 n53
O'Driscoll, Robert, xiii
O'Flaherty, Liam, 87
Olivier, Lawrence, 117 n27
Olson, Elder, 110 n22
O'Neill, Maire, 112 n59
Oshima, Shotaro, 126 n48

Parkinson, Thomas, 108 n7, 108 n8
Peacock Theatre (at the Abbey Theatre), xii, 56, 63, 70, 90-2, 123 n31
Pearse, Padraic, 88
Phoenix Theatre, Dublin, 122 n17
Pickard-Cambridge, A.W., 119 n45
Pinter, Harold, 94
Pirandello, Luigi, 97 n13, 124 n37
Poel, William, 34, 64-5, 105 n91, 118 n33
poetic drama (London experimental theatres), xi, 91-3
Pound, Ezra (see also Fenollosa manuscript), xii, 32-3, 35-7, 45, 54, 60-1, 105 n91, 107 n5, 114 n76, 114 n80
Price, Nancy, 93
Purcell Operatic Society, 13

Qamber, Akhtar, xiii

Raine, Kathleen, xiii, 117 n26, 123 n30
Rambert, Ballet, 92
Rambert, Marie, 91-2
realism (see naturalism)
Reinhardt, Max, x, 65-8, 77 106 n92, 111 n41, 116 n17
Ricketts, Charles, ix, 16, 36-7, 42, 108 n11
Reynolds, Lorna, xiii
Robinson, Lennox, 98 n27, 119 n35
Rougement, Denis de, 98 n26
Royal Court Theatre, London, 101 n18
Ruddock, Margot, 93

Index

Russian Ballet, 16, 65, 84, 92, 101 n21, 106 n92
Ruth Taylor Theatre, San Antonio, Texas, 111 n41

Saddlemyer, Ann, 97 n11, 99 n31, 100 n15, 101 n31, 118 n32
Sadler's Wells Company, 92
Schechner, Richard, 111 n41
Scott, Michael, 123 n31
Serlio, Sebastiano, ix, 101 n29
Shakespeare William, 58, 59, 65, 81, 93, 94, 101 n28, 101 n31, 106 n92-3, 108 n11, 114 n80
Sharp, Cecil, 105 n91
Shaw, George Bernard, xi, 3
Shaw, Martin, 101 n23
Shelley, Percy Bysshe, 97 n12, 98 n18, 109 n14
Sherrard, Philip, 123 n30
Sickert, Oswald, 42, 108 n6
Sidnell, Michael J., xiii, 103 n48
Skelton, Robin, 97 n11
Skene, Reg, xiii
Smith, Carole H., 112 n56
Smith, D. Travers, x
Smith, Jean and Arnold Toynbee, 118 n29
Smith, William Robertson, 119 n47
Society of the Theatre, The, 105 n91
Sophocles (see W. B. Yeats's versions of *King Oedipus* and *Oedipus at Colonus*)
Speaight, Robert, 115 n2
Stage Society, The, 15, 92, 112 n59, 118 n32
Stanislavski, Constantin, 59, 101 n28, 101 n31, 105 n91

Stratford Ontario Festival Players, 117 n27
Strindberg, August, xi, 1
Symons, Arthur, 4, 115 n10, 115 n12, 118 n29
Synge, John Millington, 2, 11, 13, 54, 75, 98 n15, 103 n53

Tairov, Alexander, 124 n37
Taylor, Richard, xiii, 46, 94, 107 n5, 109 n21, 111 n32, 122 n25, 125 n45
Theatre of Dionysus, Athens, 121 n5
Théâtre Libre, Paris, 99 n30
Thorndike, Sybil, 63, 76, 118 n34
Tsukimura, Reiko, 112 n55

Ure, Peter, xii, 23, 109 n15, 112 n46

Valois, Ninette de, xi, 56, 84-6, 89-93, 121 n11, 122 n25, 123 n36
Vendler, Helen, 109 n15, 110 n32, 111 n36
Vitruvius, 66

Wagner, Richard, 66, 115 n10
Waley, Arthur, 108 n6, 110 n24
Whistler, James McNeill, 61, 114 n76
Whitehead, A.N., 80
Wilde, Lady, 23, 103 n54, 104 n70
Wilde, Oscar, 88
Willett, John, 121 n13
Williams, Raymond, 109 n20, 110 n22

Wilson, F.A.C., 108 n7, 109 n15, 111 n36, 112 n48, 112 n53, 116 n20, 122 n25, 123 n30
Woodruff, Graham, 121 n5
Worth, Katharine, xiii, 59, 94, 125 n39, 125 n47
Wright, Frank Lloyd, 111 n41

Yeats, Jack B., ix, 37, 105 n91
Yeats, W.B., 'Another Song for a Fool', 105 n89
  'Art and Ideas', 61
  At the Hawk's Well, 36-41, 49, 84
  'Baile and Aillinn', 98 n20
  'The Ballad of Father Hart', 19
  'Byzantium', 24
  Calvary, 43, 49-53
  The Cat and the Moon, 86, 94
  Cathleen ni Houlihan, 2, 54, 86
  'Certain Noble Plays of Japan', 41
  The Countess Cathleen, 2, 11, 13, 16, 18, 20-2, 23, 24, 34, 102 n37-8, 104 n80, 107 n4
  'Crazy Jane Grown Old Looks at the Dancers', 90
  The Death of Cuchulain, 94-5
  Deirdre, 4-11, 19, 34, 38, 40, 56
  Diarmuid and Grania, 3
  Diary, 7, 8, 59
  'Discoveries', 3, 24, 32, 44, 80
  The Dreaming of the Bones, 43, 53-5, 86, 91
  'Edmund Spenser', 14
  'Ego Dominus Tuus', 79

Fighting the Waves, 84-6, 90, 93
Four Plays for Dancers, 42, 83-4
A Full Moon in March, 90, 93
The Golden Helmet, 4, 102 n43
The Green Helmet, 4, 34, 94, 102 n43
The Herne's Egg, 93, 94
'The Hosting of the Sidhe', 89
The Hour-Glass, 4, 13, 15, 16, 18, 23-32, 34, 93, 102 n37
The King of the Great Clock Tower, 86-91
King Oedipus (based on Sophocles' play), xi, 28, 56, 63-4, 74-8, 80
The King's Threshold, 4, 36-7, 104 n78
The Land of Heart's Desire, 3, 13, 18-20, 32, 102 n37-8
'Modern Ireland, an Address to American Audiences', 86-8
'The Moods', 44
Oedipus at Colonus (based on Sophocles' play), xi, 56, 63-4, 74, 78, 80-2
On Baile's Strand, 4, 25, 36-7, 39-40, 83-5, 95, 102 n43
The Only Jealousy of Emer, 43-7, 49, 84
'A People's Theatre', 60
Per Amica Silentia Lunae, 44, 45, 47, 79-80
The Player Queen, 1, 13, 56-60, 93-4
The Pot of Broth, 93
Purgatory, 94

Index

Responsibilities, 11, 30
The Resurrection, 63-4, 68-74, 80-1, 89, 91, 93
'The Reform of the Theatre', 15
'Sailing to Byzantium', 78
'The Second Coming', 24
The Shadowy Waters, 4, 16
'The Song of the Old Mother', 19
'The Stolen Child', 19
'theory of the Mask', 8, 58-9
'The Three Hermits', 32

The Tower, 78
'The Tower', 78
'The Tragic Generation', 3
'The Tragic Theatre', 35
The Wanderings of Oisin, 7
Where There is Nothing, 15, 101 n18, 118 n32
Words Upon the Window-Pane, 56
A Vision, 63, 68, 73, 78, 81

Zeami (see also Japanese Noh drama), 41-2, 107 n5